19 NEBRASKA

35-110

THE BEEF STATE

# *Classic* AMERICAN *Cars*

# QUENTIN WILLSON

# *Classic* AMERICAN *Cars*

*Photography by*
**Matthew Ward**

## DK PUBLISHING, INC.

## A DK PUBLISHING BOOK

**PROJECT EDITOR**
PHIL HUNT
**ART EDITOR**
KEVIN RYAN
**EDITOR**
JILL FORNARY
**DESIGNER**
CLARE DRISCOLL
**MANAGING EDITOR**
FRANCIS RITTER
**MANAGING ART EDITOR**
DEREK COOMBES
**DTP DESIGNER**
SONIA CHARBONNIER
**PICTURE RESEARCHER**
SAM RUSTON
**PRODUCTION CONTROLLERS**
RUTH CHARLTON, ROSALIND PRIESTLEY
**US EDITOR**
MARY SUTHERLAND

First American Edition, 1997
2 4 6 8 10 9 7 5 3 1

Published in the United States by DK Publishing Inc.,
95 Madison Avenue, New York, New York 10016

Visit us on the World Wide Web at
http://www.dk.com

Copyright © 1997 Dorling Kindersley Limited, London

Text copyright © 1997 Quentin Willson

**Library of Congress Cataloging-in-Publication Data**

Willson, Quentin.
Classic American Cars / by Quentin Willson. -- 1st American ed.
p. cm.
Includes index.
ISBN 0-7894-2083-X
1. Automobiles--United States. I. Title.
TL23.W583 1997
629.222 ' 0973--dc21                                        97-16172
                                                              CIP

Color reproduction by Colourscan, Singapore
Printed and bound in Belgium

**NOTE ON SPECIFICATION BOXES**
Every effort has been made to ensure that the information
supplied in the specification boxes is accurate. Unless otherwise indicated,
all figures pertain to the actual model in the specification box.
A.F.C. is an abbreviation for average fuel consumption.

# CONTENTS

# FOREWORD
## *J.D. Power*

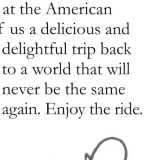

AMERICAN CARS HAVE TAKEN A BAD RAP over the past half century. Yet, for all the criticisms, it's fair to say that the American motor industry brought us the things we love most about the automobile.

American cars gave us electrically adjustable seats, windows, and mirrors, automatic transmission, air-conditioning, two-tone paint, and Wonder Bar radios. More recently, they've provided us with remote buttons to lock and unlock the doors, airbags, and catalytic converters. They might not be highly regarded for engine efficiency, pin-sharp handling, or stunning looks, but, when it comes to delivering what customers want in an easy and reliable package, American cars have always led the world.

Aficionados may balk at accepting the cardinal role that US iron has played in the development of today's reliable, safe, comfortable, and convenient machines, but they should read this book with an open mind. Many of the innovative automotive features we take for granted originated in American cars. A technological history that started back in 1911 with the development of the electric starter fast-forwards through this book's pages to today's symbol of convenience – the cup holder.

Now is the perfect time, as we near the millennium, to look back at the evolution of America and her cars and reflect on her contribution to the advancement and refinement of the automobile. Quentin Willson's nostalgic look at the American classic car is for most of us a delicious and delightful trip back to a world that will never be the same again. Enjoy the ride.

J.D. POWER III
CHAIRMAN OF J.D. POWER ASSOCIATES

# AUTHOR'S PREFACE

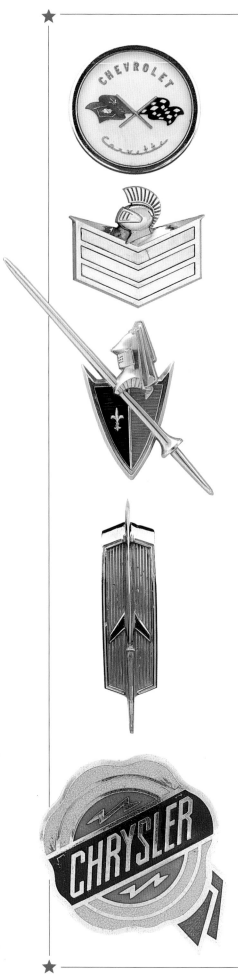

IT WAS THE LONG, HOT SUMMER of '69 that did it. I was a wide-eyed English 11-year-old at grade school in a small town 50 miles outside of Chicago. Dad was doing a sabbatical year lecturing at the local University, and I was having the time of my life driving in American cars.

I'd fallen in with a kid called Nicky, whose father owned the biggest GM dealership in Illinois. Their vast clapboard house sat in 10 acres with a huge yard strewn with Pop's trade-ins. There'd be lines of cast-off 'Cudas, Firebirds, Caddys, and Continentals, and each with the keys temptingly hidden under the sun visor. Nicky was the sort of kid my parents had spent months warning me against, which is why I liked him on sight. He could tell a 260 V8 from a 289 with his back turned, and he'd spend hours explaining about hemi-heads and Positraction. I was a mightily impressed 11-year-old.

And that year was what really got me into cars. Every day after school I'd cycle up to Nicky's place and we'd borrow a Fairlane, a Mustang, or an Eldorado and practice power slides and handbrake turns. Nobody wanted old muscle cars, and every week Nicky's Dad would bring home yet another load of heavy metal. Boss Mustangs, Coronet Hemis, Chevelle SSs, Pontiac GTOs: we drove them all. I owe Nicky a big debt of gratitude. He showed a shy English kid in short pants two of the wildest things in life: America and American cars.

This book is a tribute to those formative years, an homage to all those wicked wheels. It's not meant to be the definitive list of best or worst, rather a nostalgic trawl through some of the most captivating and compelling cars ever.

# THE MOST INFLUENTIAL CARS IN THE WORLD

1951 CHRYSLER IMPERIAL

FOR THE BEST PART OF THREE decades the world has snickered up its sleeve at American cars. To listen to the torrent of ridicule, you'd think Detroit's offerings of the Forties, Fifties, and Sixties were designed by madmen on their way to the asylum. The British sneered at their unseemly girth, weight, and size; the Germans mocked Motown's build quality; and the Italians would rather have walked than commit stylistic suicide behind the wheel of a Cadillac Eldorado. Even some Americans joined the chorus of dissenters. John Keats in *The Insolent Chariots* remarked with rancor that "American automobiles are not reliable machines for reasonable men, but illusory symbols of sex, speed, wealth, and power for daydreaming nitwits." Only the French, bless them, actually reckoned a Pontiac Parisienne was glamorous enough for posing on the Périphérique. But were American motor cars as dire as the pundits said? Were they really that ridiculous?

Perhaps jealousy is the word we're looking for. America's prosperity

**IKE ARRIVES IN STYLE**
*In November 1952, an impressed world watched Dwight Eisenhower celebrate his election to the presidency of the most powerful nation on earth in a shining Lincoln Capri Convertible the size of a small house.*

in the postwar years was all spangled exuberance and cheerful opulence. While Europe trundled about in dumpy little gray-and-black boxes with all the charisma of church pews, Americans squealed around in glittering, pastel-colored rocketships. Europe was winding her windows down by hand, while Americans were operating not just their windows but their seats, trunk releases, and transmissions at the touch of a chromium-plated button. The nearest Europeans got to American cars was on the flickering screen. We envied all those lantern-jawed heroes who could one-hand huge Chevrolets around corners while smoking a cigarette and still manage to feign an expression of complete and utter boredom.

**1949 CADILLAC SERIES 62**
*While Europe was filling in the bullet holes and struggling to rebuild her devastated cities with money borrowed from America, Americans were tooling around in dreamboats like the '49 Cadillac.*

Power-sliding never looked so easy or so much fun. The cars we watched in the movies seemed to be built on the same grand scale as the stars who drove them and, if we'd been honest, we would have cut off bits of our anatomy just to sit in the passenger seat. Americans were living the good life through their cars, and Europe's resentment was nothing more than old-fashioned envy.

## Keeping the Customer Satisfied

In retrospect, the cars that Detroit rolled out in the three decades after World War II were shining stars of the world's automotive firmament. This was the most imaginative and fertile period of car design ever, when every stylistic sleight of hand, and then some, was used in the deepest and most inventive examination of the consumer psyche by any industry in the history of the world. Simply put, American automobiles defined the vernacular of the modern motor car. They not only gave us panoramic windscreens, two-tone paint, and whitewalls but also those little touches that mean so much, like cruise controls, air-conditioning, AM/FM radios, power windows and seats, not to mention automatic transmission and power steering.

In 1959, the buyer of a Chevrolet Impala was faced with an embarrassment of riches of factory and dealer-installed optional equipment.

### HARLEY J. EARL
#### 1893–1969

HARLEY EARL, GM's chief stylist, was the man who shaped millions of American cars. "You design a car so that every time you get in it's a relief – you have a little vacation for a while." The first motor mandarin to really understand that consumers don't buy cars with their heads but their trousers, Harley Earl invented automotive attitude.

In 1956, Earl headed GM's state-of-the-art $125 million Tech Center and led a styling team of 1,200 people. Every year they took automotive design over the edge and back again. In the chain of command, Earl was somewhere between God and

HARLEY J. EARL

President, without the latter's limitations. GM's corporate culture elevated stylists over engineers, who were relegated to the role of rude mechanics employed to turn Earl's whims of steel into production realities. In his tenure at GM, Harley Earl took the solemnity out of the American car and replaced it with a chromium smile.

EARL'S PROTOTYPE LE SABRE SHOW CAR BOASTED A CONVERTIBLE TOP THAT CLOSED AUTOMATICALLY WHEN IT SENSED RAIN

**1954 CHEVROLET CORVETTE**
*The '54 drastic plastic Corvette is a perfect example of Earl's stylistic audacity. He knew there was a whole raft of buyers out there bursting for some automotive bravado, so he layered on the charisma with a trowel.*

The order form listed 78 different accessory choices ranging from a Super Turbo-Thrust V8, Positraction rear axle, and Turboglide automatic transmission, through power steering, brakes, windows, and seats, to electric rear-tailgate glass on station wagons. The roster of comfort and vanity options offered was even longer. Consumers could enrich their lives with de luxe steering wheels, shaded rear windows, air-foam seat cushions, tri-volume horns, simulated wire-wheel covers, tissue dispensers, Magic-Aire heaters, tinted Soft Ray glass, and Strato-Rest headrests. The culture of convenience was running riot.

By the time the Mustang appeared in mid-'64, Ford had turned the option list into an arcane art form. Not only could you choose from a whole hill of engines, transmissions, and axles but there were now specially named generic option groups to

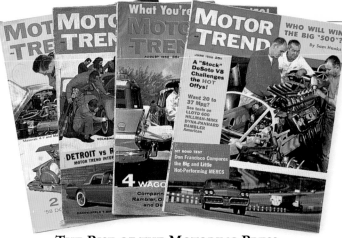

**THE RISE OF THE MOTORING PRESS**
*By the mid-Fifties, the public was obsessed with automobile styling, and the shape of cars to come was a national gambit. The newsstands groaned with auto magazines, and GM was spending $162 million a year on advertising to persuade consumers to debauch themselves with tail fins.*

consider. The GT Equipment Group, the Handling Package, the Rally Pack, the Visibility Group, and the Interior Decor Group were all part of the pony car building-block philosophy: give buyers a sexy-looking car as a platform and allow them to customize it to their own individual specifications. Not for nothing did the Ford ads trumpet "Mustang – Designed To Be Designed By You." With so many options available, the San Jose factory could literally churn out an entire year's Mustang production without any two cars ever being exactly the same.

## Power to the People

Transatlantic metal gave the world much more than just chrome and creature comforts. American cars also gave us fun in the form of the ever-higher numbers at the tips of their speedometer needles. Detroit's horsepower gallop began in '51 when Chrysler let loose its 180 bhp Fire-Dome V8.

## —RAYMOND LOEWY—
### 1893–1987

RAYMOND LOEWY DESIGNS REPRESENT the articulation of plenty that hallmarks postwar America. He shaped everything from pencil sharpeners, Studebakers, the interior of Skylab, and Coca-Cola dispensing-machines to the inside of JFK's official jet, Air Force One.

Many of Loewy's creations have become foundation stones of modern design; the Studebaker Avanti of '63, the Coldspot refrigerator, the Greyhound Scenicruiser bus, and the Hallicrafter radio all illustrate his key contribution to American design. His motoring credits include the Studebaker Commander, Starliner, Golden Hawk, and Champion. A maverick to the last, he reckoned design was "far too important to be left in the careless hands of company men in suits." He will be remembered as one of the prime architects of the American Dream.

LOEWY DESIGNED COCA-COLA DISPENSER

LOEWY AND HIS FAMILY POSE BY THE SENSATIONAL AVANTI

THE '57 STUDEBAKER GOLDEN HAWK

**MOTORAMA**
*GM's Motoramas were the wildest car shows ever conceived. Regularly pulling up to two million visitors, there were dancers, actors, musical stage shows, and amazing displays of postwar technical prowess. From 1949 to 1961, they showcased new products and were GM's most powerful weapon in the marketing war.*

**FUTURISTIC CHASSIS**
*The gadget-laden '57 Mercury Turnpike Cruiser was hailed as "space age design for earth travel." Apart from a chassis like the Brooklyn Bridge, it had Air Cushion suspension and push-button automatic transmission.*

This was followed by Chevy's small-block V8 of '55. Five years later, the Chrysler 300F was stampeding out 400 bhp, and by '63 a Hi-Po T-Bird was displacing 427 cubes and red-lining the dynamometer at a jaw-dropping 425 bhp. Then in '66 Chrysler went ballistic with their 426 Hemi, firing the first serious salvo of the performance war that was to send horsepower ratings spiraling through the stratosphere. The heat had been turned up to the max, and by the late Sixties a super-warm Chevy Chevelle SS was pumping out a thundering 450 bhp.

Those were the days when anyone with enough bucks could saunter into their local showroom, check all the right boxes on the options list, and find themselves master of absolutely apocalyptic horsepower. They were mass-produced cars that, in a straight line, could run bumper-to-bumper with handcrafted Ferraris, Jaguars, and Aston Martins. Today those performance figures are impressive enough, but back then they were heart-stoppingly quick. Even the monikers were enough to hurry the hormones. Eliminator, Marauder, Cougar, Cyclone, Thunderbolt, and Charger were machines that could accelerate to 60 in the time it took to say their

names. The world's greatest democracy really did offer power to the people, and it came in the wrapping of the muscle car. Never had so much heave been available to so many for so little.

## Behind a Painted Smile

Automotive historians may claim that Europe was more technically audacious with its unitary bodies, radial-ply tires, and four-wheel drive. Certainly the British pioneered disc brakes and fuel injection, the Germans perfected millimetrically precise build quality, and the Italians made V12 engines almost reliable. But Detroit could come up with plenty of wizardry too. Look at some of the show cars, particularly from GM's Motoramas, and you'll see that innovation was not only being actively pursued, it was in rude health. These cars were plugged up like the Pentagon, with transistorized electrical systems, magnesium bodies, automatic transaxles, special tiny engines to drive accessories, TVs instead of rearview mirrors, and even gas turbine engines. Harley Earl's 1951 Le Sabre, named after the F-86 jet fighter, stood no higher than a mailbox, had built-in automatic jacks for changing wheels, and a power-operated convertible top that automatically raised when it sensed rain on the console.

**1957 CADILLAC COUPE DE VILLE**
*The '57 Coupe de Ville came with air-conditioning as standard. In Britain, the amount of buildings with air-con could be counted on the fingers of one hand.*

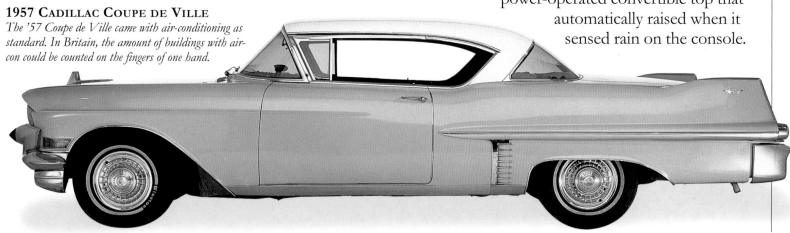

**POWER BRAKES**

*Stopping a Detroit dinosaur took some effort, and by the mid-Fifties most cars had power drum brakes as an option. As the picture shows, power-assisted brakes were meant to help "the lady."*

**POWER WINDOWS**

*Electric windows appeared in the late Forties and, by 1955, were de rigueur. This was an age when almost every minor control was designed to be activated by a dainty finger.*

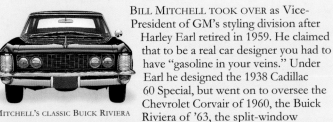

## BILL MITCHELL
### b.1912

MITCHELL'S CLASSIC BUICK RIVIERA

BILL MITCHELL TOOK OVER as Vice-President of GM's styling division after Harley Earl retired in 1959. He claimed that to be a real car designer you had to have "gasoline in your veins." Under Earl he designed the 1938 Cadillac 60 Special, but went on to oversee the Chevrolet Corvair of 1960, the Buick Riviera of '63, the split-window Corvette Sting Ray of '63, the Oldsmobile Toronado of '66, and the Chevrolet Camaro of '67. He admired clean, sculptured lines and rejected the bosomy, rounded shapes favored by Earl.

In the 1970s he bemoaned the blandness of Detroit's offerings. "They all look alike. I have to read the goddam badges to know what they are." After his retirement, Mitchell still rode a Yamaha 1000 motorbike and enjoyed a much modified Pontiac Trans Am powered by a Ferrari Daytona engine.

MITCHELL WITH HIS MAKO SHARK SHOW CAR, WHICH WAS SAID TO BE HIS ALL-TIME FAVORITE DESIGN

Mercedes, 47 years later, has just gotten around to using rain sensors to actuate the windshield wipers on their E-Class range.

In 1959, GM touted its Firebird III at the New York and Boston Motorama shows. Billed as "Imagination In Motion," it had an ultrasonic key that you aimed at the door, a cockpit pre-heater, a formed plastic interior, and the steering wheel, transmission lever, brake, and throttle were all worked from a single joystick control. The Whirlfire GT 305 regenerative gas turbine unit developed 220 bhp through a differential-mounted gearbox and De Dion transaxle. Braking was courtesy of an aluminum drum antilock system with a grade retarder on the differential. This was wildly futuristic gadgetry that in 1959 must have seemed as if it came straight out of the pages of *Buck Rogers and the Forgotten Planet*. Behind the revolving stage shows and the pageantry, Motoramas showed America and the rest of the world that the white-coated eggheads in GM's technical labs were slipstreaming a vapor-trail into the future. Against Detroit's backdrop of prodigious innovation, the European motor industry's efforts looked almost tame.

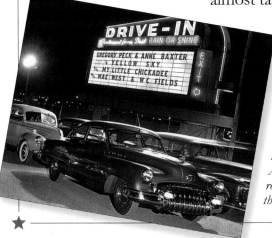

**DRIVE-IN MOVIES**

*In 1955, Detroit rolled out eight million new cars, and teenagers with after-school jobs were a perfect target market. The automobile allowed youth to escape the middle-aged morality of Main Street America and savor the romance and passion of the drive-in.*

## Sultans of Style

But the Big Three auto manufacturers – GM, Chrysler, and Ford – knew that technical features alone wouldn't move metal. What buyers wanted was street-strutting style, and nobody supplied dash and flash like Uncle Sam. The postwar American Dream was founded on the concept of "populuxe," or luxury for all. By the late '50s, the average Chevrolet or Buick was groaning under the weight of 44 lb (20 kg) of twinkling chrome and luxury add-ons. In 1949, Harley Earl's finny Cadillac was considered the last word. By '55, its styling motifs had percolated to even the humblest Chevy. Fins, sweepspears, and the two front-end protuberances known as Dagmars gave customers an extra receipt for their money, and sales of new cars in '55 totaled $65 billion, or 25 percent of the Gross National Product. Americans were willing, even grateful, to spend vast amounts of money on two-and-a-half tons of candy-pink space rocket simply because it transported them into another world.

**GLIMPSE OF THE FUTURE**
*The Firebird II, III, and XP-21 were all GM show cars displayed at the Motorama exhibitions of the Fifties. Incredibly futuristic, they boasted technical wizardry like automatic steering sensors and gas turbine engines.*

**SPACE CULTURE**
*Space-age styling metaphors were plastered over the Fifties American car. Speed, rocket ships, and outer space became the national narcotic.*

Despite what the sceptics would have us believe and behind all that gratuitous glitz were some of the world's most significant cars. You simply can't deny the huge influence of creations like the Mustang, Corvette, Jeep, GTO, and Thunderbird. They were pioneering designs that changed the shape and styling of cars forever. And every last one of them was conceived and built in America. Europeans may have been envious, but they were quick enough to mimic what they saw. By the Sixties, the British had two-tone Vauxhall Crestas, finned Zephyrs and Zodiacs, sweepspears on Sunbeam Rapiers, and quad headlights on Rolls-Royces. The French pasted Detroit's styling cues onto the Simca Aronde, Vedette, and Facel Vega, and even the Germans couldn't claim they weren't occasionally inspired. In 1961, Mercedes launched their four-door 190 sedan. Teutonic perfection incarnate maybe, but what were those two weird little flourishes on the rear? Dainty little tail fins. The world's oldest car maker had publicly admitted that when it came to style, Detroit

had taught all there was to know. The influence of America's auto stylists was incredibly far-reaching, and there wasn't a car company in the world that didn't cull something from Motown's awesome aesthetic arsenal.

Britain might have been first with the sports car and Italy the coupe, but America came up with machines that could literally be all things to all men. Reacting exactly to what the market wanted, Detroit fielded the personality car. Thunderbirds, Rivieras, Cougars, Barracudas, Camaros, and Firebirds were brilliant niche products that offered consumers cars that were distinctive and separate. One ad for the Dodge Challenger promised "a car you buy when you don't want to be like everyone else." And by offering a raft of options longer than the Gettysburg Address, Dodge was telling the truth.

**1957 DODGE CUSTOM ROYAL**
*Dodge's '57 model range had a lowered silhouette, "Swept Wing" styling, and taillights that looked like jet-engine afterburners. The F15 jet fighter in the background was meant to reinforce the tenuous relationship between car and plane.*

sculptors in steel and visionaries driven from within. One contemporary said of Earl: "He was like a Roman Emperor in Constantinople. Nobody in the history of industry ever had such an incredible effect over man-made objects like Earl." Raymond Loewy, creator of the Studebaker Avanti, also designed streamlined trains and the Lucky Strike cigarette pack. Loewy once said, "Pride, social consciousness, and the desire to serve mankind better are the only inspirations a designer needs." History will rank luminaries like these as the grand masters of design who between them changed the face of 20th-century consumer culture irreversibly. They gave the American car its dazzle and swagger; they lowered, lengthened, and widened it, gave it half a hundred stylistic metaphors, more glass than a greenhouse, and pushed the envelope of design to its absolute limit. They gave the automobile optimism and hope. They made it a machine that promised unlimited possibilities.

Bucket seats, mag wheels, center consoles, and various instrument packs all gave buyers more choice than there were atoms in the universe. The Ford Mustang was the world's fastest-selling car, not because it was dynamically special but because its appeal was wider than that of any other car before or since. And Motown's trick of piling on the personality undeniably influenced everything from the Ford Cortina to the BMW 3-Series. The modern cult of auto individuality began in the US.

## Gurus of Glitz

One reason why American cars of the period were so remarkably influential was the quality of their designers. Men like Harley Earl, Raymond Loewy, Lee Iacocca, Bill Mitchell, and Virgil Exner were

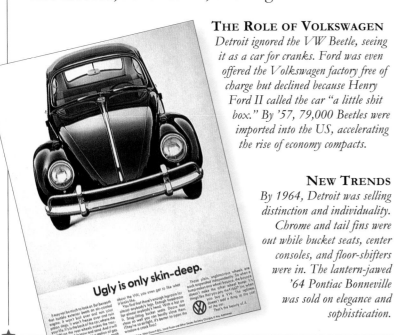

**THE ROLE OF VOLKSWAGEN**
*Detroit ignored the VW Beetle, seeing it as a car for cranks. Ford was even offered the Volkswagen factory free of charge but declined because Henry Ford II called the car "a little shit box." By '57, 79,000 Beetles were imported into the US, accelerating the rise of economy compacts.*

**NEW TRENDS**
*By 1964, Detroit was selling distinction and individuality. Chrome and tail fins were out while bucket seats, center consoles, and floor-shifters were in. The lantern-jawed '64 Pontiac Bonneville was sold on elegance and sophistication.*

**GLAMOUR AT THE TOP**
*The baby boomers of the Sixties bought US iron in vast numbers. John and Jackie Kennedy personified the new-age Camelot dynasty and swept around in glamorous Lincoln Continental Convertibles. With a matinee idol as President, life took on the excitement of a Hollywood movie.*

## LEE A. IACOCCA
### b.1925

IACOCCA'S ORIGINAL PONY LOGO

LEE IACOCCA IS WIDELY regarded as the father of the greatest automotive success in postwar history, the Ford Mustang. As Ford's precocious General Manager in 1961, the 36-year-old Iacocca came up with the idea of a sporty compact to woo the burgeoning youth market. He reasoned that if the performance of a car like the Corvette could be stuffed into an affordable car for the masses, it would sell like hotcakes. And it did.

The Mustang remains the world's fastest-selling car; by its first birthday, it had racked up nearly half a million sales. It was the first of the pony cars, a breed of two-door personal coupes that went on to wow America for the best part of 20 years. Without Iacocca's vision, determination, and tenacity, one of the world's most memorable cars might well have remained just a doodle on the back of an envelope.

IACOCCA IS SEEN AS THE "FATHER" OF THE MUSTANG

And America's preoccupation with how things looked wasn't just self-obsessed narcissism, it helped keep the machinery of mass consumption turning. Good design was the American Way and a million miles from Europe's puritanical austerity of line. This was the great liberal phase of American styling, and it flourished because it was essential to the nation's economic health. Yearly model changes, or what Harley Earl chose to call "dynamic obsolescence," guaranteed not only an annual orgy of buying but also the less affluent could purchase last year's cast-offs at used-car prices. The designer anticipated the public's desires and kept his creations just an arm's length away, so the buyer always had next year's model to look forward to, yet another dream to pursue.

## Dreaming Out Loud

For three decades, Detroit fueled a massive metallic fantasy that Americans believed in and the rest of the world desired. And it was a fantasy engineered by a deliberate corporate policy of encouraging dreams. Detroit invented the "dream car" at a moment in American history when the future looked bright, exciting, and almost close enough to touch. American cars looked the way they did because that was the way America looked. Scholars who trawl through the social history of the United States could do worse than study her cars, because American automobiles tell us more about America's past than a whole library of history books ever could.

**ORIGINAL MUSCLE**
*John DeLorean, Pontiac's Chief Engineer, shoe-horned the division's biggest V8 into the timid little Tempest, creating one of the first muscle cars, the Pontiac GTO. It was an instant hit with speed-thirsty youngsters.*

After World War II, America didn't have a single bomb crater anywhere, and the '49 Roadmaster mirrored a population looking forward to a brave new world of plenty. The happy and handsome '55 Chevrolet Bel Air epitomized the confident consumption of the Fifties boom years, while the baroque '59 Cadillac revealed a nation so near to satiety that it had forgotten the itch of desire. By 1960, America was losing her arrogance, and the austere and anxious 1962 Chevy Corvair reflected a society in the grip of paranoia. While Vietnam and race riots raged, the belligerent Dodge Charger R/T of 1968 betrayed a country at war with itself. After the fat and glittery Fifties and Sixties dreamboats came the lean and hungry Chevrolet Vegas and Ford Pintos. And by the time the abstemious and severe Cadillac Seville debuted in 1975, the dream had evaporated completely. And that's maybe the most fascinating and compelling thing about watching American cars. They've always precisely mirrored the highs and lows of the American Way.

## Uniquely American

The cynics should remember that while it's easy to snicker at machines that turned dreams into dollars, it's even easier to lose sight of the purity of vision, the genius, and the humanity that made Detroit's tremendous achievements possible. American cars may have been continually satirized for the vice of flamboyance, but it was exactly that florid styling that gave them their greatest virtue. It blessed them with a genuinely

**GLAMOROUS AND FUN**
*This Chrysler 300X research car is being tried out by the 1966 Miss World. Even though the extreme experimentation of the Fifties had gone, research projects still offered publicity for manufacturers in the Sixties.*

hopeful, twinkling innocence. And it doesn't matter that all those strident Oldsmobiles, DeSotos, and Plymouths didn't obey European strictures of order and elegance. They had an infectious optimism and cheer that actually made Americans feel better about themselves and the nation they lived in; Detroit was selling a welcome distraction from heartbreak. As Virgil Exner once said, "A well-styled car will make a man feel better at the end of his journey than when he started." For 30 years the American automobile hasn't only entertained millions of Americans, it's given the rest of the world a unique glimpse behind the curtain of the American Dream. Motown's glory years may have gone, but they'll never be forgotten.

**1966 FORD MUSTANG**
*This milestone car was born halfway through 1964 and continues to this day. If any car sums up the spirit of American auto manufacturing, it must be the Mustang. In automotive history no other car has flown from the showrooms faster than Ford's pony prodigy.*

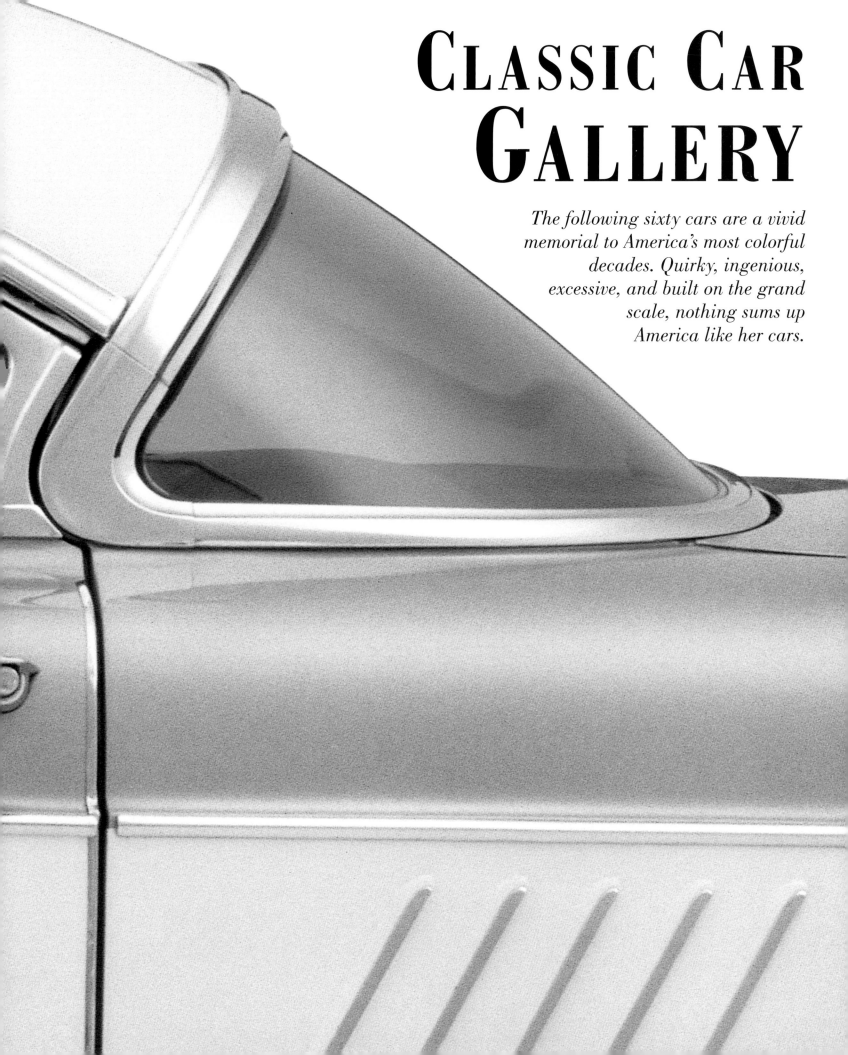

# CLASSIC CAR GALLERY

*The following sixty cars are a vivid memorial to America's most colorful decades. Quirky, ingenious, excessive, and built on the grand scale, nothing sums up America like her cars.*

# The Forties

*America's intervention in World War II filled the nation with a self-confidence that would fertilize phenomenal postwar industrial growth. The automobile industry never had it so good.*

CHRYSLER'S 25TH ANNIVERSARY MODEL WAS THE FIRST ALL-NEW POSTWAR STYLING CHANGE

MODERN AMERICA began in 1945. Postwar austerity didn't last long, and by the late Forties American workers produced 57 percent of the world's steel, 60 percent of the oil, and 80 percent of all the cars on the planet. In the five short years after the end of the war, Americans were able to buy electric clothes dryers, long-playing records, Polaroid cameras, frozen foods, and automatic garbage-disposal units. It was a brave new world of miracle materials like plastics, nylon, Styrofoam, vinyl, and chrome. What had once seemed science fiction was suddenly everyday life.

The GI Bill of Rights in 1945 invigorated the economy and stimulated education, industry, and business, kick-starting the biggest consumer boom the world has ever seen. Houses for heroes became a national priority and, between 1945 and 1950,

15 million shot up all over America. The Levitts of Levittown fame could build one in just 16 minutes, charging $7,990 for a four-and-a-half room, two-story with central heating, refrigerator, washing machine, and an eight-inch Bendix television set. Marriage rates soared and American newlyweds

**1941 LINCOLN ZEPHYR V12**
*Lincoln's '41 Zephyr V12 carried over many prewar styling elements. Tall, long, and boxy, it wasn't until 1942 that it got a mild facelift. The last prewar Lincoln rolled out of the factory on February 10 the same year.*

| | 1940–1945 | 1946 | 1947 | 1948 | 1949 |
|---|---|---|---|---|---|
| **AUTOMOTIVE** | • Streamlining percolates down even to lowly **Chevrolet**s<br>• Harley Earl and design team view P-38 Lightning pursuit plane<br>• Supercharged **Graham** is fastest car powered by side-valve six<br>• **DeSoto** builds fuselage sections for the Martin B-26<br>• **Chrysler** resumes car production in 1945 | • 50th Anniversary of US car industry<br>• **Ford** is biggest manufacturer, producing 468,022 cars<br>• Steel strike and shortage of materials affect car industry<br>• **Lincoln** Continental is pace car at Indianapolis 500<br>• **Mercury** launches Sportsman Convertible with wood body panels<br>• **Pontiac** dusts off pre-war Silver Streak styling | • **Chevrolet** now America's No. 1 car maker with 671,546 cars<br>• **Frazer** and **Kaiser** are first US cars to exhibit new postwar styling with unbroken lines<br>• Virgil Exner designs new enclosed-body **Studebaker** Champion<br>• **Pontiac** builds a rear-mounted straight-eight engine<br>• Woodie look is all the rage<br>• Whitewall tires now available<br>• Henry Ford dies | • **Cadillac** brings out dramatic new 62 Series with dorsal fins<br>• **Hudson** launches famous "Step-Down" body<br>• **Pontiac** introduces Hydra-Matic automatic transmission<br>• Rare and radical **Tucker** Torpedo unveiled<br>• Charles Nash dies<br>• **Willys** launches the Jeepster, America's last true touring car | • **Ford** returns to the top spot, making an extraordinary 1,118,308 cars<br>• **Buick** debuts new Roadmaster<br>• **Chevrolet** makes first major restyle since the war<br><br>1949 HUDSON SUPER SIX |
| **HISTORICAL** | • Japanese bomb Pearl Harbor (1941)<br>• First US troops land in Europe (1942)<br>• US miners strike (1943)<br>• Eisenhower masterminds D-Day (June 6, 1943)<br>• Glenn Miller disappears over English Channel (1944)<br>• A-bomb on Hiroshima (1945)<br><br>GENERAL DWIGHT D. EISENHOWER | • United Nations holds first session<br>• IBM introduces electronic calculator<br>• First subsurface atomic explosion at Bikini Atoll<br>• Ten Nazi war criminals executed at Nuremburg<br>• *Road to Utopia* opens with Bob Hope and Bing Crosby | • Marshall Plan offers massive aid for postwar Europe<br>• US crusade against Communism begins<br>• Soviets test A-bomb<br>• Plutonium is discovered<br>• John Cobb sets land speed record of 394 mph (634 km/h)<br>• Bell XI plane breaks the sound barrier at over 600 mph (965 km/h)<br>• Rita Hayworth divorces Orson Welles | • Soviets blockade Berlin, and their envoy to the UN walks out<br>• Truman wins Presidency<br>• Transistor is invented<br>• Kinsey Report on American sexual mores is published<br>• Kansas ends prohibition<br>• Tennessee Williams wins Pulitzer Prize for *A Streetcar Named Desire*<br>• George Orwell publishes *1984*<br>• Norman Mailer publishes *The Naked and the Dead* | • Berlin blockade ends<br>• Truman says he won't hesitate to use the A-bomb again but publicly tries to calm "red hysteria"<br>• Einstein publishes Theory of Gravitation<br>• Actor Robert Mitchum jailed for smoking marijuana<br>• RCA launches new system for broadcasting color TV pictures<br>• 7" vinyl records first available |

**1948 LINCOLN CONTINENTAL COUPE**
*Although largely unchanged from 1946 models, the $4,662 '48 Continental was considered one of the most glamorous cars you could buy at the time. The Metropolitan Museum of Modern Art selected it as one of the eight automotive "works of art." Time magazine also ranked it in their top 10 of 100 best-designed products.*

**RITA HAYWORTH'S CONTINENTAL**
*Movie star Rita Hayworth had the necessary $2,812 to buy one of only 850 '41 Lincoln Continentals, as did architect Frank Lloyd Wright who described it as "the last classic car built in the United States." This was one of the final cars produced before the US entered the war.*

flocked to the suburbs. Precisely nine months after VJ-Day, the cry of the baby rang out across the land; by the end of '46, 3.4 million had been born. Radio shows like *The Adventures of Ozzie and Harriet* portrayed a cozy domestic idyll of plenty and normalcy. In 1948, some 172,000 American households each paid $200 to buy a television set. By 1950, 7½ million families were glued to the tube. And, looking through that new window on the world, American expectations grew grander and grander.

## The Rebirth of the Industry

Clearly, the nation now needed a different kind of mobilization. In steel-starved 1945, new car sales totaled just 69,500. By 1949, this had risen to a staggering 5.1 million. Buyers were so desperate to own new Chevys and Fords that they not only paid full list price but slipped the dealer a fan of dollars to jump the line. An ad for the 1945 model Buick featured a shimmering car emerging from a gloomy scene of war. The copy read, "Buicks are for the lively, exciting, forward-looking world so many have fought for." In a *Saturday Evening Post* article titled "Your Car After the War," a man called Harley Earl prophetically predicted low, futuristic machines with curved windshields and slipstream bodies.

Although the metal in showrooms after 1945 was mainly a prewar lunch warmed over, aerodynamic styling and technical advancement gradually seeped into the brochures. Two significant engineering developments dominated the decade: the V8 engine and the automatic gearbox. It was General Motors that pioneered a generation of V8s, along with the seminal Hydra-Matic and Dynaflow self-shifters. Innovation was everywhere, not least in Preston Tucker's spectacular helicopter-engined Tucker Torpedo of 1948.

But it was Harley Earl who came up with probably the greatest automotive innovation of the late Forties, the infant fin. His '48 Cadillac wore two strange little bumps on its rear, and from that point the vernacular of the postwar American automobile was defined. Cars would never be mere transportation again.

**1947 CHRYSLER TOWN AND COUNTRY**
*Chrysler's Town and Country series of 1947 was a new departure from prewar designs. Wood had previously been used only on station wagons, but the T & C Sedan had unique wood-bodied sides.*

# 1943 WILLYS
## *Jeep MB*

WILLYS LOGO ON THE
ENGINE BLOCK

AS ONE WAR CORRESPONDENT said, "It's as faithful as a dog, as strong as a mule, and as agile as a mountain goat." The flat-fendered Willys Jeep is one of the most instantly recognizable vehicles ever made. Any American TV or movie action hero who wasn't on a horse was in a Jeep. Even General Eisenhower was impressed, saying "the three tools that won us the war in Europe were the Dakota and the landing craft and the Jeep."

In 1940, the American Defense Department sent out a tough spec for a military workhorse. Many companies took one look at the seemingly impossible specification and 49-day deadline and turned it down flat. The design that won the contract and made it into production and the history books was a mixture of the ideas and abilities of Ford, Bantam, and Willys-Overland. A stunning triumph of function over form, the Jeep not only won the war but went on to become a cult off-roader that's still with us today. The Willys Jeep is surely the most original 4x4 by far.

PRESIDENT-ELECT EISENHOWER VISITING
TROOPS IN KOREA IN 1952

### ENGINE
Power came from a Ford straight four, which took the Jeep to around 60 mph (96 km/h), actually exceeding US Army driving regulations. The hardy L-head motor developed 60 bhp, and the Warner three-speed manual box was supplemented by controls allowing the driver to select two- or four-wheel drive in high or low ratios.

QUICK-RELEASE
CLUTCH
DISENGAGES
ENGINE FAN
FOR FORDING
STREAMS AND
RIVERS

### DUAL-PURPOSE HEADLIGHT
The headlight could be rotated back to illuminate the engine bay.

### FRONT VIEW
Earlier Jeeps had a slatted radiator grille instead of the pressed steel bars shown here. The silhouette was low but ground clearance high to allow driving in streams as deep as 21 in (53 cm). Weather protection was vestigial.

LEFT-HAND SUSPENSION SPRINGS HAD A STIFFER
RATING TO COPE WITH THE WEIGHT OF THE ENGINE

DORCAS

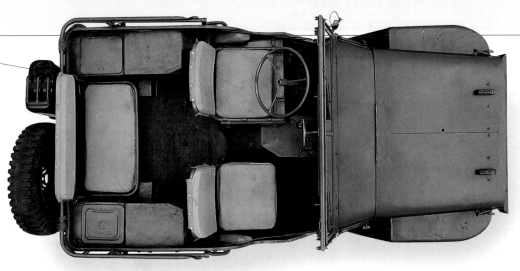

READY FOR ANYTHING, JEEPS CAME WITH GAS CAN, SHOVEL, LONG-HANDLED AX, AND GRAB BARS

## EXTENDED LIFESPAN

The Jeep was a brilliantly simple engineering solution to the problem of rugged mobility at war, but the life expectancy of an average vehicle was expected to be less than a week! In practice, many have survived to this day.

### ─ SPECIFICATIONS ─

**MODEL** 1943 Willys Jeep MB
**PRODUCTION** 586,000 (during World War II)
**BODY STYLE** Open utility vehicle.
**CONSTRUCTION** Steel body and chassis.
**ENGINE** 134cid straight four.
**POWER OUTPUT** 60 bhp.
**TRANSMISSION** Three-speed manual, four-wheel drive.
**SUSPENSION** Leaf springs front and rear.
**BRAKES** Front and rear drums.
**MAXIMUM SPEED** 65 mph (105 km/h)
**0–60 MPH (0–96 KM/H)** 22 sec
**A.F.C.** 16 mpg (5.7 km/l)

## EXPOSED COLUMN

Driver safety wasn't a Jeep strong point. Many GIs ended up impaled on the steering column even after relatively low-speed impacts. Only the generals fought the war in comfort, and Jeeps were strictly no frills. Very early Jeeps had no glove compartment.

## WHAT'S IN A NAME?

Jeeps were first called General Purpose cars, then MA, and finally standardized as MB, but to this day nobody's sure from where the unofficial Jeep name originated. Some say it is a phonetic corruption of GP, or General Purpose, others that it was named after a curious little creature called Eugene the Jeep who appeared in a 1936 Popeye cartoon.

HAND-OPERATED WINDSHIELD WIPERS

DOORS WOULD HAVE ADDED WEIGHT, SO SIDE STRAPS WERE A TOKEN GESTURE TOWARD DRIVER SAFETY

FIRST PRODUCTION JEEP MODEL, THE MA, HAD A COLUMN CHANGE

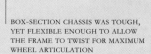

BOX-SECTION CHASSIS WAS TOUGH, YET FLEXIBLE ENOUGH TO ALLOW THE FRAME TO TWIST FOR MAXIMUM WHEEL ARTICULATION

HIGH CLUTCH, NARROW FOOTWELL, AND UNMOVABLE SEAT FORCED A DRIVING POSITION WITH KNEES SPLAYED

# EVOLUTION OF THE JEEP

THAT THE LEGENDARY quarter-ton Jeep was in fact a mishmash of available components virtually thrown together at record speed is amazing enough. But no one could have predicted that it would eventually create a whole new market for lifestyle leisure vehicles. Willys was to survive into the Fifties and Sixties, but investment was lacking until Chrysler acquired Jeep in the Eighties. Now the brand is in the ascendancy and giving rival Land Rover some stiff opposition.

## 1942

WILLYS AND FORD JEEPS saw service in every theater of war, and the two versions were almost identical. By August 1945, when wartime production of the Jeep ended, the two companies together had manufactured over 600,000 Jeeps. The US Army continued using Jeeps well into the Sixties, and some European armies still use them now.

### KEY FEATURES
• Wartime Jeeps used the L-head straight four from production cars of the early '40s
• Willys bid lowest for the Jeep contract, but the Defense Department included Ford
• Tiny Bantam company produced 3,000 Jeeps

## 1950

WILLYS WAS QUICK to identify a burgeoning domestic market, so they cleaned up their warhorse and marketed it in a more civilized guise. One of the first civilian Jeeps, the Jeepster Phaeton, was introduced in 1948–49 and sold well in its opening years. This 1950 model sported a revised grille and improved engine, but sales fell by over 60 percent.

### KEY DEVELOPMENTS
• High-compression 7.0:1 cylinder head option available
• Split windshield rigid with chrome edging
• Mechanically operated soft-top
• Rear wheels gain fenders

WILLYS TRIED TO broaden the Jeep's appeal by bringing out a small Jeep-based station wagon. It was a longer car, built on the same wheelbase, and sold from 1946 to 1951. All were painted maroon with wood trim and had dual wipers, front bumper guards, and rails. Six-cylinders had wheel trim rings, cigarette lighter, and whitewalls.

### KEY DEVELOPMENTS
• Restyled grille is divided by five horizontal bars
• New center gauge dashboard design and wrap-around rear bumper
• The first Jeep with a single-piece windshield

# 1943 WILLYS *Jeep MB*

**WAR HERO**
World War II made the Jeep's reputation – it was used in every theater of war in which GIs served, and appears in this poster recruiting soldiers to fight in China.

**JOINT EFFORT**
Of the 135 manufacturers contacted by the Defense Department, only Willys and Bantam rose to the challenge. Ford presented their version some time later.

THE JEEP MAY HAVE HAD COMPETENCE AND CHARISMA, BUT IT ALSO HAD A PRODIGIOUS THIRST FOR FUEL

DAMPING IS BY LEAF SPRINGS AND HYDRAULIC SHOCKS WHICH GIVE A SURPRISINGLY GOOD RIDE

## 1962

JEEP PREDATED the Range Rover by a decade with its oversized, go-anywhere four-wheel drive station wagon. With ample room for at least five and a massive luggage deck, it became a favorite of intrepid outdoor types. Trim levels could be specified, marking the Jeep's most significant departure from its utilitarian military image.

### KEY DEVELOPMENTS
• Called the Wagoneer, this new Jeep was all-new in a market all on its own
• Gladiator pickup available
• Willys name was dropped in 1963 and changed to Kaiser-Jeep Corporation

## 1971

BY THE MID-SIXTIES, manufacturers were seeing a new all-terrain leisure market emerge. International Harvester launched the Scout, and Ford joined in with the Bronco. Lacking real investment, Jeep based a new car, the Jeepster Commando, on the Wagoneer's wheelbase. A roadster, station wagon, and convertible were offered.

### KEY DEVELOPMENTS
• Five engines offered, from a 134cid four to a 304cid V8
• Press acclaims new Jeeps, saying "passenger comfort is way above average"
• Jeepster had a 101 in (257 cm) wheelbase

## 1976

BASED ON JEEP'S hefty Cherokee station wagon, the Honcho was the company's big pickup for the Seventies. The most popular engine was the V8. Jeep got the luxury sport utility vehicle ball rolling with the full-size Cherokee, but it wasn't until the compact four-door models were introduced that sales really took off.

### KEY DEVELOPMENTS
• AMC acquires Kaiser-Jeep Corporation and becomes largest 4x4 manufacturer in US
• Range Rover's success in the UK expands the off-road market

## 1994

AFTER YEARS OF SUCCESS with the smaller Cherokee, Jeep came up with the larger and more luxurious Grand Cherokee in the mid-Eighties. With every possible luxury, it was strong competition for the big Japanese 4x4s and now-legendary Range Rover. Priced competitively, it was adopted as a very practical suburban trinket.

### KEY DEVELOPMENTS
• Jeep now a division of the Chrysler Corp.
• Grand Cherokee with V8 now has 125 mph (201 km/h) performance
• Antilock braking system (ABS), low-emission engine, and air-conditioning are added

### EASY ACCESS
The Jeep's hood was held down using quick-release sprung catches. The upper catch held the fold-down windshield.

### TRENDSETTER
Those stark fenders and large all-terrain tires may look humble and functional, but the Jeep's claim to fame is that it spawned utility vehicles from Nissans and Isuzus to Discoverys and Range Rovers.

### JEEP FIREPOWER
The Jeep remains very popular with fans of military memorabilia, especially in its various specialty guises. This archive shot – taken in Germany – shows a Jeep equipped with a potent antitank cannon.

LONG-STROKE SIDE-VALVE FLAT-TOP FOUR DEVELOPED PLENTY OF STUMP-PULLING TORQUE

AXLES ARE FULLY FLOATING WITH BENDIX-WEISS, RZEPPA, OR SPICER CONSTANT VELOCITY JOINTS

# 1948 TUCKER
## *Torpedo*

EXTRAVAGANT ORNAMENTATION

THERE'S NO OTHER POSTWAR CAR that's as dramatic or advanced as Preston Tucker's futuristic '48 Torpedo. With four-wheel independent suspension, rear-mounted Bell helicopter engine, pop-out safety windshield, and uncrushable passenger compartment, it was 20 years ahead of its time.

"You'll step into a new automotive age when you drive your Tucker '48," bragged the ads. It was a promise that convinced an astonishing 300,000 people to place orders, but their dreams were never to be realized. Problems with the engine and Tuckermatic transmission, plus a serious cash-flow crisis, meant that only 51 Torpedos left the Chicago plant. Worse still, Tucker and five of his associates were indicted for fraud by the Securities Exchange Commission. Their acquittal came too late to save America's most eccentric car from an undignified end.

### HOLLYWOOD PORTRAYAL
The 1988 film *Tucker: The Man and His Dream* starred Jeff Bridges and told a none-too-accurate story of an impassioned genius thwarted by Detroit's Big Three. In reality, Tucker failed because the project was underfunded.

### FAMILY CREST
The horn on the steering wheel lay flush for safety, and was adorned with the Tucker family crest in injection-molded acrylic, suggesting a Cadillac-type bloodline.

### INTERIOR
Some say Detroit conspired to destroy Tucker, but steering wheels on Torpedos were from the Lincoln Zephyr, given freely by Ford as a gesture of help. Although the interior was groaning with safety features, the Tucker sales team felt that it was too austere.

REAR LIGHT, LIKE MUCH OF THE TUCKER, WAS BOUGHT IN AND WAS A PREWAR DODGE DESIGN

REAR ENGINE WAS PLACED CROSSWISE ON THE OVERHANG BETWEEN THE TWO INDEPENDENTLY SPRUNG REAR WHEELS

VENTS WERE TO REDUCE THE CONSIDERABLE ENGINE HEAT

## LOW PROFILE

One of the fastest cars on American roads, the Tucker had a low floor that gave it a huge aerodynamic advantage. The roof tapered in two directions to reduce lift forces, and the drag coefficient was as low as 0.30. The Torpedo's top speed was 120 mph (193 km/h), and an astonishing 30 mpg (10.6 km/l) was possible.

## AN INSTANT HIT

The public loved the Tucker not only for its comfort, power, and safety but also because the styling was completely free from the usual prewar clichés. The prototype was ready in 60 days, and more than 5,000 people attended the launch.

WHEN THE TUCKER WAS PREVIEWED TO THE PRESS, THE FRONT BUMPER WAS MADE OF WOOD

DARING CYCLOPS HEADLIGHT SWIVELED WITH THE FRONT WHEELS

STEERHORN BUMPER GAVE THE CAR A DRAMATIC FRONT VIEW

### SPECIFICATIONS

**MODEL** 1948 Tucker Torpedo
**PRODUCTION** 51
**BODY STYLE** Four-door sedan.
**CONSTRUCTION** Steel body and chassis.
**ENGINE** 335cid flat six.
**POWER OUTPUT** 166 bhp.
**TRANSMISSION** Three-speed Tuckermatic automatic, four-speed manual.
**SUSPENSION** Four-wheel independent.
**BRAKES** Front and rear drums.
**MAXIMUM SPEED** 120 mph (193 km/h)
**0–60 MPH** (0–96 KM/H) 10.1 sec
**A.F.C.** 30 mpg (10.6 km/l)

## ENGINE

The first Tucker engine was a monster 589cid aluminum flat six that proved difficult to start and ran too hot. It was replaced by a 6ALV 335cid flat six, developed by Air-Cooled Motors of Syracuse. Perversely, Tucker later converted this unit to a water-cooled system.

WITH NO ENGINE UP FRONT, LUGGAGE SPACE WAS COMMODIOUS

SLIPPERY FRONT WAS DESIGNED TO CLEAVE THE AIR

# THE CAR OF THE FUTURE HELD BACK IN THE PAST

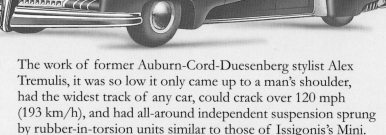

ARTWORK OF A PROTOTYPE 1947 TUCKER TORPEDO

PRESTON TUCKER WAS AN EXTRAORDINARY automotive maverick. An unlettered engineer whose favorite phrase was "our boss is bigger than all of us, and it's the automobile," he was a well-connected wheeler-dealer who'd made a fortune from the design of a gun-turret mounting for World War II bombers. Obsessed by a dream of building the most advanced passenger car in the world, he secured a lease on a vast plant in Chicago, previously used to build engines for Boeing Superfortresses. A born deal-maker, he'd shrewdly raised $8 million franchising 1,800 Tucker dealerships before his automotive vision of the future was even in running prototype form.

The Torpedo was so different from anything else on four wheels that it was a complete sensation.

PRESTON TUCKER

The work of former Auburn-Cord-Duesenberg stylist Alex Tremulis, it was so low it only came up to a man's shoulder, had the widest track of any car, could crack over 120 mph (193 km/h), and had all-around independent suspension sprung by rubber-in-torsion units similar to those of Issigonis's Mini.

But the much-vaunted 589cid helicopter power plant was a nightmare, as was the troublesome Tuckermatic transmission, which was later replaced by a modified Cord gearbox. Tucker's tribulations soon leaked out to the press, who'd heard that prototypes sent to dealerships were plagued with glitches.

# 1948 TUCKER
## *Torpedo*

REAR DEFROSTER WAS ONE OF ONLY FOUR OPTIONS AVAILABLE

INTERIOR WAS DESIGNED BY AUDREY MOORE, WHO HAD WORKED WITH RAYMOND LOEWY ON STUDEBAKERS

NOVEL ENGINE WAS POSITIONED LOWER THAN THE REAR PASSENGER SEAT TO DIMINISH NOISE, HEAT, AND FUMES

**HELICOPTER HELL**
The early 589cid modified helicopter engines were a bit of a disaster. One test driver, Gene Haustein, described them as "slow as the moon coming up, making a noise like a barrel full of monkeys with the lid propped open."

PRESTON TUCKER DEMANDED A "SASSY" REAR END FROM HIS DESIGN TEAM

Tucker

MANUFACTURER
1  5
ILLINOIS 48

The situation got worse. Tucker had raised capital by a conventional stock market issue, but he ran afoul of the Securities Exchange Commission because the production cars didn't include all the audacious technical features he'd listed in his prospectus: direct fluid drive, disc brakes, sealed cooling system, electronic ignition, and fuel injection. The suits from Wall Street claimed that the cars being offered to the public did not fulfill Tucker's grandiose promises. The Tucker Corporation was therefore guilty of fraud.

After an essential $30 million loan was refused, Tucker was forced into voluntary liquidation. The tragedy was that Tucker could have sold every car he made, and he even had a float of several million dollars in the bank. The Chicago plant closed in the summer of 1948, by which time 37 Torpedos had been produced. In the end, volunteer workers assembled another 14 cars from remaining parts.

PRESTON IN HIS DREAM CAR

TUCKERS WAIT OUTSIDE COURT DURING THE TRIAL

Fifty-odd years later, the Torpedo remains one of America's most charismatic classics, and mint specimens can sell for up to $300,000. Many are proudly exhibited in museums, and some have even racked up a quarter of a million miles without incident. The Torpedo was meant to herald the brave new world of postwar America but failed because it was too complicated, too daring, and too under-resourced. A perfect example of American automotive genius, Tucker's precocious prodigy was guilty of just one sin – it bloomed too soon. Five years later the story might have been very different.

## UNIQUE AND EXCITING

The front was like no other American car, with a fixed circular headlight lens that pivoted with the steering and a front panel that blended artfully into the bumper and grille.

FRONT AND REAR SEAT CUSHIONS COULD BE INTERCHANGED TO SPREAD WEAR AND TEAR

SEAT BELTS WERE NEVER INSTALLED BECAUSE THEY WERE THOUGHT TO SUGGEST THAT THE CAR WAS UNSAFE

RADIO WAS AN OPTIONAL EXTRA

THE TORPEDO WAS ONE OF THE FIRST WIDE-TRACK CARS AND HAD EXCEPTIONAL CORNERING ABILITY

THE TORPEDO COULD BRAKE TO A STOP IN HALF THE DISTANCE OF AN AVERAGE CAR

# 1949 BUICK
## *Roadmaster*

THE '49 ROADMASTER TOOK the market's breath away. With a low silhouette, straight hood, and fastback styling, it was a poem in steel. The first Buick with a truly new post-war look, the '49 was designed by Ned Nickles using GM's new C-body. It also boasted two bold new styling motifs: Ventiports and an aggressive 25-tooth "Dollar Grin" grille. Harley Earl's aesthetic of aeronautical entertainment worked beautifully, and Buick notched up nearly 400,000 sales that year. Never mind that the windshield was still two-piece, that there was no power steering, and the engine was a straight eight – it looked gorgeous and came with the new Dynaflow automatic transmission. The Roadmaster, like the '49 Cadillac, was a seminal car and the first flowering of the most flamboyant decade of car design ever seen.

GUN-SIGHT HOOD DECORATION

**DASHBOARD**
The instrument panel was new for '49 and described as "pilot centered" because the speedo was positioned straight ahead of the driver through the steering wheel. The design was taken straight from Harley Earl's Buick Y-Job.

**REAR LIGHT CLUSTER**
The Art Deco taillights looked upscale and blended smoothly into the rear fenders. Nobody could have guessed that they were emergent fins that, in 10 years, would mushroom to almost comical proportions.

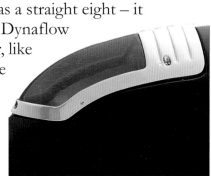

**VENTIPORTS**
Open Ventiports were sealed mid-year because a high-school principal complained that male students used those on his Roadmaster to relieve themselves.

SPOTLIGHT WITH MIRROR WAS A $25 OPTION

VENTIPORTS GAVE THE IMPRESSION OF A FIRE-BREATHING JET ENGINE

Roadmaster

BUICK

ELEGANT FLOURISH
COMPLETES THE SWOOPING
TEAR-DROP REAR

LESS
EXPENSIVE
BUICKS HAD
ONLY THREE
VENTIPORTS,
BUT THE
LAVISH
ROADMASTER
SPORTED
FOUR

## RAISED PROFILE

The Roadmaster may have
shared its body with the
Oldsmobile 98 and the Cadillac
Series 62, but it gave Buick a
distinction never seen before.

## NEW AUTOMATIC

Dynaflow automatic
transmission was
introduced in 1948 as
an option on the Roadmaster.
By '49 it had become standard
equipment on the Series 70 Roadie
and an immensely popular option on
Series 50 and, later, Series 40 models.

ENGINE WAS
FITTED WITH
HYDRAULIC
"LASH-ADJUSTER"
THAT KEPT EACH
OF THE 16 VALVES
CORRECTLY SET
AND SILENCED

ALTHOUGH DIVIDED BY A
CENTER PILLAR, WINDSHIELD
GLASS WAS CURVED

### SPECIFICATIONS

**MODEL** 1949 Buick Roadmaster
Series 70
**PRODUCTION** 18,415
**BODY STYLE** Two-door
fastback coupe.
**CONSTRUCTION** Steel body
and chassis.
**ENGINE** 320cid straight eight.
**POWER OUTPUT** 150 bhp.
**TRANSMISSION** Three-speed
Dynaflow automatic.
**SUSPENSION** Front and rear
coil springs.
**BRAKES** Front and rear drums.
**MAXIMUM SPEED** 100 mph
(161 km/h)
**0–60 MPH** (0–96 KM/H) 17 sec
**A.F.C.** 20 mpg (7 km/l)

THE ROADMASTER BEGAN
THE TREND FOR LOWER,
SLEEKER STYLING

THE GM C-BODY HAD
CLOSED QUARTERS
AND SEDANETTE
STYLING

## ENGINE

The Roadie had a Fireball straight-eight cast-iron 320cid engine
that always started with a roar because the starter switch
was connected to the accelerator and engaged
by depressing the pedal all the way to
the floor. The Fireball pushed out 150
ponies and breathed through
Stromberg or Carter carbs.

DYNAFLOW WAS SUCH
A NEW IDEA THAT
BUICK PROUDLY
SCRIPTED
IT ONTO
THE REAR
FENDER

TIRES WERE
820x15
WHITEWALLS

# EVOLUTION OF THE BUICK ROADMASTER

FOR YEARS GM'S COPYWRITERS crowed that "when better cars are built, Buick will build them," and in a sense that hyperbole was true. In its day, the gloriously voluptuous Roadmaster was a serious set of wheels, only one step down from a Cadillac, and to own one meant you had really arrived. Big, bold, and brash, the '49 was perfect for its time. Optimistic, opulent, and glitzy, it carried flamboyant styling cues that told people a block away that this was no ordinary car – this was a Buick; even better, the very best Buick money could buy.

AD FOR THE 1956 ROADMASTER
STRESSED THAT IT WAS THE
"BUICK OF BUICKS"

## 1945–46

THE FIRST POSTWAR Buicks were practically unchanged from 1942, with engines that dated back to 1936 and chassis frames that originated in 1933. But they did have all-coil suspension and Harley Earl styling, and the Roadmaster Convertible was Buick's fastest and most glamorous car. Buick did well in '46, producing more than 156,000 cars.

### KEY FEATURES
• Permi-Firm steering on all models
• Two-tone instrument panel with wood grains
• Only three-speed manual transmission available
• Standard vacuum-operated windshield wipers

## 1953

IN '53 THE ROADMASTER gained the first Buick V8, nicknamed the "Nail-Head" because of the small diameter of its valve heads. The nose was shortened to accommodate the smaller lump, and power steering, power brakes, and Dynaflow drive became standard. This was Buick's 50th anniversary, celebrated by the seven millionth Buick built.

### KEY DEVELOPMENTS
• New V8 engine goes into 50 percent of all Buicks
• Calendar year production total tops 485,000
• Dynaflow gets twin turbines, which increases torque by 10 percent
• 80 percent of Buicks have Dynaflow

# 1949 BUICK
## *Roadmaster*

**A CAR TO ASPIRE TO**
Roadmaster was a brilliant name for the top-of-the-line Buick and soon became the preferred choice of professionals who couldn't quite make it to Cadillac territory.

PRISMATIC REARVIEW
MIRROR WAS AN
OPTIONAL EXTRA

THE '49 ROADIE
WAS THE PUREST
AND MOST BEAUTIFUL
BUICK EVER MADE

| 1955 | 1957 | 1991 | 1994 |
|------|------|------|------|

A MAJOR FACE-LIFT for '55 didn't do much for the Roadmaster. The vertical grille bars were replaced by a tight mesh, and the body styling was distinctly slab-sided. The Ventiports and hood ornaments stayed, but the result was a much blander machine. The public cared not, buying nearly 800,000 Roadies to put Buick in industry third place.

**KEY DEVELOPMENTS**
- Gold-colored Roadmaster desk script and hood ornament
- Convertible gets standard leather
- 10 choices of interior trim
- Eight-millionth Buick rolls off the line

LOWER AND SMOOTHER, with a more dramatic sweepspear that kicked up violently over the rear wheel arch, the restyle of '57 made the Roadmaster look a lot like every other American car. Gone was that chaste individuality, and Buick began to lose its reputation as a maker of high-quality cars. Production was down 24 percent.

**KEY DEVELOPMENTS**
- Revised front suspension with ball-joint mounting
- Grille reverts to vertical bars
- New two-piece torque tube
- New engine mountings
- Nine-millionth Buick hits the showroom

BUICK RESURRECTED the Roadmaster name for 1991 after a foolish and inexplicable 33-year hiatus. Riding on a body-on-chassis design dating back to '77, the '91 Roadmaster was a shadow of its former self. Long, heavy, and ungainly, it bore too obvious a resemblance to other GM products and had completely lost all character.

**KEY DEVELOPMENTS**
- Roadmaster name first appears on aero-look eight-passenger station wagon
- Fuel-injected 5.0 V8
- Driver's-side airbag and ABS standard
- Improved suspension gives better stability
- Same chassis and mechanicals as Chevrolet Caprice

THERE WERE ONLY minor changes to the Roadmaster in '94, the main one being the optional Corvette-based 260 bhp V8. The rear-drive sedan and station wagon continued, and stock power was from the 5.7 V8. This year's models returned only 16 mpg (5.7 km/l) in urban driving. Alas, the once great name had been sacrificed on the altar of badge engineering.

**KEY DEVELOPMENTS**
- Station wagons get rear-facing two-place third seat and vista roof
- Solar-Ray tinted windshield
- Improved sound deadening
- Lockout switch for power windows
- Sedan roof pillars hinder visibility

**LOUD AND PROUD**
The center of the steering wheel was one of five places where Dynaflow was written on the car. The steering itself was unassisted and required a hefty five turns lock-to-lock.

INTERIOR FABRICS WERE PLUSH, WITH A CUSTOM TRIM OPTION

FULL-WIDTH BENCH SEATS WERE STANDARD ON THE '49 ROADIE

**BUICK STYLING**
Gun-sight hood ornament, bucktooth grille, and Ventiports were flashy styling metaphors that would become famous Buick trademarks.

# 1949 CADILLAC
## *Series 62*

THE CADILLAC SCRIPT IS FAMOUS THE WORLD OVER

WE OWE A LOT TO the '49 Cadillac. It brought us tail fins and a high-compression V8. Harley Earl came up with those trendsetting rear rudders and John F. Gordon the performance motor. Between them they created the basic vernacular of the postwar American car.

In 1949 the one millionth Caddy rolled off the production line, and the stunning Series 62 Fastback or Sedanette was born. Handsome and quick, with Hydra-Matic transmission, curved windshield, and hydraulically operated front seats and windows, it was a complete revelation. Everybody, including the haughty British and Italians, nodded sagely in admiration and, at a whisker under $3,000, it knocked the competition dead in their tracks. As Cadillac ads boasted: "The new Cadillac is not only the world's most beautiful and distinguished motor car, but its performance is a challenge to the imagination." The American Dream and the finest era in American cars began with the '49 Cadillac.

## BENTLEY CONNECTION

THE CLASSIC 1952 BENTLEY R-TYPE Continental certainly bears a startling similarity to the '49 Cadillac. Motoring academics have frequently hinted at plagiarism, suggesting that the Bentley's comely teardrop shape was inspired by Harley Earl's design. Naturally, the boys at Bentley declined to comment, but nonetheless the two cars do display an uncanny kinship of line. However, far from waving writs about, Earl, Cadillac, and GM took a philosophical approach and simply smiled quietly to themselves. For after all, we all know that imitation is the most sincere form of flattery.

1952 BENTLEY R-TYPE CONTINENTAL

GLORIOUS TAPERING ROOF LINE MADE DUMPY EUROPEAN CARS LOOK LIKE CHURCH PEWS

**CADILLAC CREST**
The V emblem below the crest denoted V8 power, and the basic badge design remained unaltered until 1952.

**BODY STYLE**
Hugely influential body design was penned by Harley Earl and Julio Andrade at GM's styling studios. Many of the '49 features soon found themselves on other GM products such as Oldsmobile and Buick.

TIRES RAN AT ONLY 24 PSI, MAKING UNASSISTED STEERING HEAVY

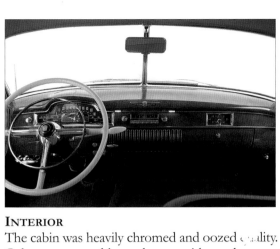

## MASCOT
The famous streamlined Art Deco goddess hood ornament first appeared after World War II and continued unchanged until 1956. America's most prestigious car wore its mascot with pride.

## INTERIOR
The cabin was heavily chromed and oozed quality. Colors were gray-blue or brown with wool carpets to match and leather or cloth seats. Steering was Saginaw, with standard four-speed auto transmission.

## ACCOLADES
British motoring journalist S.C.H. Davis rated the '49 one of the six outstanding cars of the two postwar decades. *Motor Trend* magazine named it "Car of the Year."

### SPECIFICATIONS
MODEL  1949 Cadillac Series 62
PRODUCTION  92,554
BODY STYLE  Two-door, five-seater fastback.
CONSTRUCTION  Steel body and chassis.
ENGINE  331cid V8.
POWER OUTPUT  162 bhp.
TRANSMISSION  Four-speed Hydra-Matic automatic.
SUSPENSION  *Front:* coil springs; *Rear:* leaf springs.
BRAKES  Front and rear drums.
MAXIMUM SPEED  100 mph (161 km/h)
0–60 MPH (0–96 KM/H)  13.4 sec
A.F.C.  17 mpg (6 km/l)

WHILE STYLING WAS SIMILAR TO THAT OF THE '48 MODEL, THE NEW OHV V8 IN THE '49 WAS AN INNOVATION

CHROME SLASHES WERE INSPIRED BY AIRCRAFT AIR INTAKES

FUEL FILLER-CAP WAS HIDDEN UNDER TAILLIGHT, A CADILLAC TRAIT SINCE 1941

## FIN STYLING
The rear fins, inspired by the Lockheed P-38 aircraft, became a Caddy trademark and would reach a titanic height on '59 models.

## EVOLUTION OF THE CADILLAC SERIES 62

'48 WAS THE YEAR of the fin and the year of the crème de la Cads. Cadillac designers Bill Mitchell, Harley Earl, Frank Hershey, and Art Ross had been smitten by a secret P-38 Lockheed Lightning fighter plane. Mitchell admitted that the P-38's fins "handed us a trademark nobody else had." Cadillac also had Ed Cole's OHV V8, some 10 years in the making. With a brief to reduce weight and increase compression, the end result was an engine with more torque and better mileage than any other at the time.

*1955 ADVERTISING BROCHURE*

### 1941

THE '41 CADILLACS had a powerful, sweeping glamour that was the envy of custom coachbuilders the world over. Hopes of returning to the wheel of a romantic '41 Series 62 Convertible kept many a GI sane. With egg-crate grille, swooping fenders, concealed gas filler, and Hydra-Matic shifting, it was the last word in modernity.

**KEY FEATURES**
• Horsepower up from 135 to 150 bhp
• New coffin-nose hood
• Optional Hydra-Matic transmission
• Record 59,572 models sold
• Genuine top speed of 100 mph

### 1947

AFTER A FOUR-YEAR consumer drought, Cadillac found itself with about 200,000 orders and only 104,000 cars. Although a warmed-over prewar design, the '46 and '47 Caddies had a sleek, wind-cheating smoothness full of rapid purpose. They were classically correct and aesthetically stunning – not bad for a car with two tons of bulk.

**KEY DEVELOPMENTS**
• First true "jellybean" body shape
• Smoothest car engine of its day
• Sombrero deep-dish wheel covers
• Modified Cadillac V crest
• Grille bars reduced from six to five

## 1949 CADILLAC
### Series 62

**BELIEVE THE HYPE**
Cadillac advertisements trumpeted that the 1949 was "the world's most beautiful car," and the simple yet elegant styling caught the public's imagination.

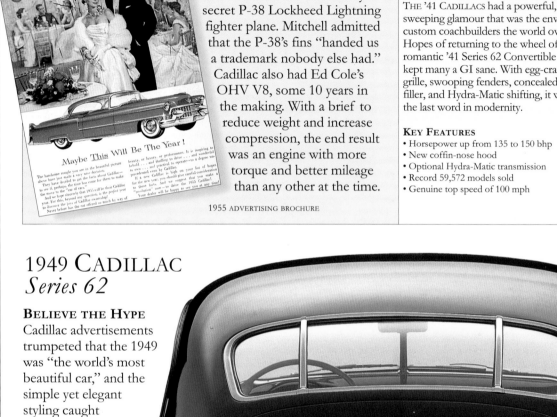

AMONG MINOR DESIGN CHANGES FROM 1948 WAS THE MORE SQUARED-OFF REAR

LG·136
NY EMPIRE STATE 57

1949 CADILLAC SERIES 62

| 1948 | 1955 | 1959 | 1961 |
|---|---|---|---|
|  |  | |  |

THE '48 CADILLAC was first to define the vernacular of the typical post-war American family sedan. A magnificent design package, it was clean, curvaceous, and beautiful, and that '49 engine was a honey. With the best styling and the finest engine in the business, Cadillac became the zenith of good taste.

**KEY DEVELOPMENTS**
- First of the fins
- First-generation modern GM OHV V8
- Class-leading economy and performance
- Distinctive fastback styling
- First luxury hardtop
- Front fender line within bodywork

'55 WAS A BANNER year for the motor industry as well as Cadillac's most successful to date, with 141,000 units built. Horsepower was up to 250 (270 in the Eldorado), and the Florentine roof was extended to sedans. Even the Dagmars were bigger, causing many complaints from other drivers savaged in parking lots.

**KEY DEVELOPMENTS**
- Eldorado has all accessories as standard except air-conditioning
- Compression ratio improved
- Redesigned egg-crate grille
- New rectangular sidelights under headlights
- Extended side molding

STRIDENT AND BAROQUE, the '59 Cadillac had ridiculously extravagant tail fins. The ultimate iron dinosaur, it was soon pilloried as proof that late Fifties America was out to lunch. But because of its flamboyance, the '59 is now a fiercely prized collector's car, with Biarritz Convertibles fetching as much as Ferraris.

**KEY DEVELOPMENTS**
- New 390cid engine
- Improved power steering
- Revised suspension
- World's highest tail fins
- 14 models in four series available

ALL '61 MODELS CAME with the 390cid, 325 bhp V8, and the new, crisp styling was inspired by GM's Bill Mitchell, who had begun to clean up the Caddy look in 1960. Family resemblance was strong, with the Series 62 hardtop coupe looking very much like the upscale de Ville, and the Eldorado Biarritz almost identical to the Series 62 Convertible.

**KEY DEVELOPMENTS**
- Rubberized front and rear coil springs replace problematic air suspension system
- Wheelbases shorter on most models
- Self-adjusting brakes from 1960 on, plus an automatic vacuum parking-brake release
- All Caddies offer lifetime chassis lubrication
- Dual exhausts no longer available

**NEW POWER UNIT**
The trendsetting new OHV 331cid V8 developed 160 bhp and weighed 188 lb (85 kg) less than the reliable but bulky L-head design. It made the '49 one of the fastest cars on the road.

CURVED WINDSHIELD WAS A NOVELTY FOR A 1949 CAR

PROTOTYPE ENGINE WAS RUN FOR 541 HOURS AND FOUND TO BE IN PERFECT CONDITION

GRILLE WAS HEAVIER ON THE '49 THAN ON THE '48, AFTER FRANK HERSHEY TOLD HARLEY EARL THAT HE DID NOT LIKE THE ORIGINAL DESIGN

LG·136
NY EMPIRE STATE 57

# 1949 PONTIAC
## *Chieftain*

STYLISH CHIEFTAIN LOGO

UP TO '49, PONTIACS looked and felt like prewar leftovers. Sure, they were reliable and solid, but they had a reputation as middle-of-the-road cars for middle-aged, middle-class buyers. Pontiac was out of kilter with the glamour boom of postwar America. 1949 was a watershed for Pontiac – the first postwar restyles were unveiled, with the new Harley Earl-designed envelope bodies trumpeted as "the smartest of all new cars." In reality, their Silver Streak styling was old hat, tracing its origins back to the Thirties. But although mechanically tame – with aged flathead sixes and eights – the '49 Chieftain Convertibles mark the transition from upright prewar designs to postwar glitz. These were the days when the modern convertible really came into its own.

### INTERIOR
A three-speed manual gearbox was standard, but Hydra-Matic automatic was available as a $159 option. There was no power steering or power brakes.

### CHIEFTAIN ORNAMENT
The Indian chief mascot never smiled, but the head was illuminated at night by a 2-watt bulb that gave a warm, yellow glow.

### REAR AXLE
*Optional rear axle ratios were Standard, Economy, and Mountain.*

### DECORATION
*The five parallel chrome bars were a Silver Streak hallmark and were aped by the British Austin Atlantic.*

### WINDSHIELD
*This was called the Safe-T-View and was one of a series of gimmicky Pontiac names that also included Carry-More trunk, Tru-Arc Safety Steering, and Easy-Access doors.*

## ENGINE
Six-cylinder engines were cast iron with four main bearings, solid valve lifters, and a puny Carter one-barrel carb. Choosing the straight eight gave you a measly extra 13 bhp but cost only $23 more. Pontiac did not offer a V8 unit in any of their models until 1955.

## SPOTLIGHTS
*Dual side-mounted spotlights were trigger-operated.*

## 1949 PONTIAC CHIEFTAIN CONVERTIBLE DE LUXE
Ads promised that "Dollar for Dollar, You Can't Beat a Pontiac," and the Chieftain was proof that Pontiac wasn't bluffing. Convertibles cost just $2,183 for the six and $2,206 for the eight and were a great bargain for the price. The engine was set well forward in a very rigid cantilever box girder frame, and the rear seat was positioned ahead of the rear axle and fender to give what Pontiac dubbed a "cradle ride."

## CHROME PANEL
*Extravagant mudguards only appeared on the De Luxe and added a classy flourish.*

## REAR BUMPER
*Intricate bumper was designed to prevent girls in full skirts from getting them caught in the bumper when opening the trunk.*

## ─ SPECIFICATIONS ─
**MODEL** 1949 Pontiac Chieftain Convertible
**PRODUCTION** Not available
**BODY STYLE** Two-door convertible.
**CONSTRUCTION** Steel chassis and body.
**ENGINE** 239cid straight six, 249cid straight eight.
**POWER OUTPUT** 90–103 bhp.
**TRANSMISSION** Three-speed manual, optional four-speed Hydra-Matic automatic.
**SUSPENSION** *Front:* coil springs; *Rear:* leaf springs.
**BRAKES** Front and rear drums.
**MAXIMUM SPEED** 80–95 mph (129–153 km/h)
**0–60 MPH** (0–96 KM/H) 13–15 sec
**A.F.C.** 15 mpg (5.3 km/l)

# The Fifties

*The postwar feel-good factor made the Fifties a decade of unprecedented leisure and prosperity. In this heady new world of television, rock 'n' roll, nuclear power, and the space race, Americans reached for the Moon.*

FAIRLANE, "THE TOUCH OF TOMORROW" IN '57

NEVER AN ERA remembered for highbrow culture, life in Fifties America did imitate art – but it was art viewed through a flickering screen. Shows like Walt Disney's weekly *Disneyland*, the *I Love Lucy* sitcom, and the *Ed Sullivan Show* changed the country's mindset. Television became a national narcotic and the tube of plenty. With seven million sets sold every year, the old order had no choice but to quietly evaporate. Television changed America's consciousness forever.

Although McCarthyism, the shadow of nuclear terror, and the Korean War dominated headlines, most Americans were busy having a good time with their bobby socks, Tupperware parties, barbecued steaks, and Billy Graham's way to God without sacrifice. These were the years of rampant consumerism, when the country binged on a

decade-long spending spree. In 1952, Americans spent $255 million on chewing gum, $235 million on greeting cards, and a staggering $23 million on mouthwash. The most stable and prosperous time in Uncle Sam's history, the Fifties promised a brave new world.

Between 1950 and 1958, the economy was riding high. Pent-up postwar demand, $100 billion worth of personal savings, the baby boom, Ike's

### ATOMIC ERA
*The nuclear specter haunted the Fifties. America regularly tested her arsenal of A- and H-bombs, in readiness for the widely anticipated confrontation with the Soviet Union.*

| | 1 9 5 0 | 1 9 5 1 | 1 9 5 2 | 1 9 5 3 | 1 9 5 4 |
|---|---|---|---|---|---|
| **AUTOMOTIVE** | • **Chevrolet** is America's No.1 car maker with 1,498,590 cars<br>• First Motorama show opens at New York Waldorf<br>• Only 333 **Volkswagen** Beetles sold in entire US<br>• First modern compact introduced, the **Nash** Rambler<br>• **Ford** wins coveted Fashion Academy award for styling<br>• **Chevrolet** offers new fully automatic Powerglide transmission | • Ford-O-Matic is **Ford**'s first fully automatic transmission<br>• **Chrysler** announces all-new 331cid hemi-head V8 for the New Yorker, plus power steering for first time<br>• *Hop Up* magazine launched, for hot-rodders and customizers<br>• Office of Price Stabilization allows some car manufacturers to raise prices<br>• One in three cars is automatic | • National steel strike and Korean War slow auto production<br>• **Buick** is third largest maker of convertibles and largest hardtop builder<br>• **Ford**'s first totally new body since 1949 features one-piece curved windshield<br>• 95 percent of all **Ford**s have V8s<br>• Office of Price Stabilization drops pegging of new car prices<br>• War cuts make whitewalls scarce | • **GM** loses $10 million<br>• **Dodge** launches famed Hemi V8 and new option, air-conditioning<br>• More chrome as war eases<br>• **Chrysler** introduces PowerFlite automatic<br><br>1953 CADILLAC ELDORADO | • **Ford** overtakes **Chevrolet** as top maker, with 1,165,942 cars<br>• Spinner hubcap becomes most popular accessory in America<br>• Harley Earl previews first Firebird experimental car at Motorama |
| **HISTORICAL** | • President Truman sanctions building of US's first H-bomb<br>• Mao Zedong and Stalin sign Mutual Defense Treaty<br>• Joseph McCarthy launches crusade against Communism<br>• First major US battle in Korea<br>• First kidney transplant<br>• Drive-in movie theaters being built at rate of 2,200 a year<br>• Nuclear test in Nevada desert<br>• *The Third Man* wins Oscar for black-and-white photography | • Average salary is $1,456 p.a.<br>• *A Streetcar Named Desire* voted best film of 1951<br>• US Atomic Energy Commission says it can produce electric power from nuclear reactors<br>• *Betty Crocker's Picture Cookbook*, first out in '50, sells its millionth copy | DWIGHT EISENHOWER CELEBRATES ELECTION VICTORY IN 1952<br><br>• Eisenhower elected President with largest-yet popular vote<br>• Contraceptive pill introduced<br>• Gene Kelly stars in *Singin' in the Rain*<br>• TWA launches tourist class air travel<br>• Nationally televised detonation of atomic bomb in Nevada desert | • Marilyn Monroe is America's favorite pinup and appears on the cover of *Playboy*<br>• Khrushchev new Communist Party leader after Stalin's death<br>• Levis are America's No.1 jeans<br>• A young Elvis Presley walks into Sun Studios, Memphis<br>• *From Here to Eternity* premieres<br>• Soviets admit they have H-bomb<br>• Cinemascope launched<br>• New "stiletto" heels panned as dangerous | • First McDonald's is born<br>• Eisenhower proposes new Interstate highway system<br>• IBM launches first computer<br>• Boeing unveil prototype 707<br>• Second H-bomb exploded at Bikini Atoll<br>• Elvis sings "That's All Right"<br>• Racial segregation outlawed in US schools<br>• Premiere of *Seven Brides for Seven Brothers*<br>• First nuclear sub launched |

**DOMESTIC UTOPIA**
*Set pieces such as this illustrated the Fifties suburban dream, with well-appointed house, Mom with her "New Look" clothes, and Dad and Junior admiring the family's shiny new 1951 Ford Custom.*

were buffed to a high sheen or swathed in chrome so a narcissistic nation could admire its reflection.

The middle-class suburbanite looked out of his window and coveted his neighbor's possessions. Success was measured in material terms – a gas barbecue, a swimming pool, a white Corvette. This credo of instant gratification changed everything, including the nation's eating habits. In 1954, Ray Kroc of San Bernadino, a high-school dropout, came up with a newfangled stand for selling French fries, soda, and 15¢ hamburgers. Today it's a fast-food empire known as McDonald's.

Interstates, and new technology meant that by the end of the decade more than 80 percent of Americans had not only electric lighting but also refrigerators, telephones, and televisions. Suburbia became a paradise of comfort and convenience, with ranch-style homes, double garages, expansive front lawns, and kitchens with a new state-of-the-art Colorama Frigidaire.

## Bright New World

Consumer durables were curvy, bosomy, and brightly colored. Buyers had had enough of the austere penury of khaki and navy blue and wanted up-to-the-minute modish pastels to show that their purchases were brand-new. Pink became the color, as worn by Elvis, Mamie Eisenhower, Cadillacs, steam irons, and even Dad's button-downs. Surfaces

**LUSHLY-UPHOLSTERED LOOKS**
*The mildly rounded 1950 Nash Rambler shows the first flowerings of curvilinear, volumetric design. By the end of the decade, an obsession with full contours would change the American car into a four-wheeled bordello.*

| 1955 | 1956 | 1957 | 1958 | 1959 |
|---|---|---|---|---|
| • Highest **Ford** output since 1923, but **Chevrolet** is back on top, producing 1,704,667 cars<br>• Big Three auto manufacturers dominate 97 percent of market<br>• US production at postwar high<br>• Auto makers agree to ban advertisements promoting performance and horsepower<br>• **Cadillac** sales peak at 141,000<br>• Chic new **Ford** Fairlane launched<br>• 60,000 foreign cars imported into US, including 25,000 **VW** Beetles | • **GM** spends $125 million on new technical center in Michigan<br>• Federal Highway Act passed<br>• Raymond Loewy blasts "jukeboxes on wheels"<br><br><br>LIMITED EDITION 1956 DESOTO ADVENTURER | • **Ford**, with all-new styling, outsells **Chevrolet** 1.67 million to 1.5<br>• New **Ford** Skyliner is world's first hardtop convertible<br>  • **Chevrolet** offers fuel injection and first 1 hp/cu in engine<br>   • Thunderbird sales up by half<br>   • Edsel launched<br>   • New magazine *Custom Cars* | • **Chevrolet** regains lead in car manufacture, with 1,142,460 built<br>• Industry-wide recession; sales worst since World War II<br>• **Chevrolet** introduces highly unpopular seat belts<br>• Thunderbirds get four seats<br>• **Ford** offers Level-Air ride for one year only<br>• 50th birthday for **Chevrolet**<br>• **GM** employs four women in their design department<br>• **Studebaker** offers compact Lark | • Virgil Exner admits that with fins he'd "given birth to a Frankenstein"<br>• Highest fins ever on 1959 Cadillac, although **Ford**, **Lincoln**, and **Mercury** fins almost disappear<br>• **Chevrolet** shows its controversial "batwing" fins<br>• **Chrysler** offers Golden Lion V8<br>• Compact **Ford** Falcon introduced<br>• Flat-six **Chevrolet** Corvair launched<br>• **Chrysler** 300D gets fuel injection<br>• Britain launches the Mini<br>• **Plymouth** Sport Fury introduced |
| • Disneyland opens in California<br>• James Dean dies in car crash<br>• New phrase "Rock 'n' Roll" coined by DJ Alan Freed<br>• 3-D movies launched<br>• *Billboard* introduces Top 100 record chart; Bill Haley's "Rock Around the Clock" is No.1 for 25 weeks<br>• Marlon Brando wins Best Actor for *On the Waterfront*<br>• Soviets test H-bomb | • Martin Luther King fights for black rights using peace<br>  • JFK goes for Vice-President nomination<br>  • Elvis buys his first pink Cadillac<br>  • First video tape shown<br>  • *My Fair Lady* opens<br>  • 60 percent of Americans are homeowners<br><br>JAMES DEAN | • USSR first in space with Sputnik<br>• Eisenhower and Nixon sworn in for second term<br>• Jack Kerouac's novel *On the Road* published<br>• Breathalyzer tested to measure alcohol on drivers' breath<br>• "Cat," "dig," "cool," "square," and "hip" enter the language<br>• Elvis in first film, *Jailhouse Rock*<br>• Bogart dies of throat cancer<br>• Jerry Lee Lewis sings "Great Balls of Fire" | • First US satellite launched<br>• Pan American World Airways begins first transatlantic flights<br>• NASA created<br>• Elvis drafted<br>• First stereo record on sale<br>• Hope Diamond donated to Smithsonian Institution<br>• *West Side Story* opens<br>• Danny and the Juniors have smash hit with "At the Hop"<br>• Last Communist newspaper, *The Daily Worker*, folds | • Fidel Castro becomes Cuban premier<br>• Nixon and Khrushchev hold "kitchen debate"<br>• First Russian rocket to reach Moon<br>• Hawaii proclaimed 50th US state<br>• Buddy Holly dies<br>• Bobby Darin wows with "Mack the Knife"<br><br><br>HULA HOOP |

**PATRIOTIC PURCHASING**
*The auto industry was the biggest player in the nation's economy, and consumers obsessed with keeping up to date were persuaded that buying a new car every year would help to build a stronger America.*

**NEW ROCK 'N' ROLL AGE**
*The name of Bill Haley's group, the Comets, echoed America's fascination with rockets and the space age. Between 1955 and 1957 their hit "Rock Around the Clock" was on the US charts for 37 weeks.*

With less time spent on cooking and eating, Americans had more time for shopping. Parents raised in the Depression had no problem swallowing the mantra that more was most definitely better. Teenagers and adults alike gorged on everything from Bill Haley records and hula hoops to cashmere sweaters, trips to Hawaii, and hot-rods. Madison Avenue spent $10 billion a year to persuade consumers that improving their lives with material possessions wasn't just okay, it was the American Way. This illusion of fulfillment was made possible by a small rectangle of plastic dubbed the credit card. Diners' Club appeared in 1950, followed by the American Express card, and by the end of the decade Sears Roebuck alone had over 10 million credit accounts.

Prosperity brought leisure, and American consumers spent $30 billion a year killing time. Sales of power tools, model kits, stamp albums, and painting sets soared. In two years Craftmaster sold Paint By Numbers sets to the value of

**MAGIC KINGDOM**
*Disneyland, opened in 1955, was like a living TV, where visitors could change channels from medieval castles to rocket ships, with souvenir shops serving as "commercials."*

$10 million and even Eisenhower was a regular dauber. For Americans wanting somewhere to go to spend time and money, the $17 million Disneyland was opened by Walt Disney on July 13, 1955, watched by 24 live ABC cameras and hosted by none other than Ronald Reagan. Two years later Disney's dream world had welcomed 10 million visitors, most of whom arrived by car.

## Freedom on Wheels

The massive American automobiles of the Fifties, although they looked like rocket-launchers with 38D cups, were built as family cars, perfect for weekend outings and vacations. As one Ford ad of the period put it, the car promised "freedom to come and go as we please in this big country of ours." A freedom from the sameness of the suburbs and the ennui of prosperity, the car became a symbol of blissful escapism.

**LOW-SLUNG PROFILE**
*By mid-decade, American cars had become so long and low that many reached only to shoulder height. The car manufacturers followed a dramatic "squashing" policy all through the Fifties, and this 1957 Mercury Turnpike Cruiser is as squat as they come. The Turnpike Cruiser boasted gadgets such as a retractable Breezaway rear window and a 49-position driver's seat.*

### HARD-SELL WITH CLASS

*Cars were sold hard on television, and Lincoln used the Ed Sullivan Show to highlight their 1955 line-up. Their elegant spokeswoman, Julia Meade, wearing an evening dress and running her gloved hands over the upholstery, was the first TV personality to be wholly identified with a single product.*

### BIZARRE CREATIONS

*By the end of the Fifties, automotive styling had become so extravagant that panning the American car became a pastime that threatened to replace baseball as a national sport. Within a few short years of its launch, this outlandish 1959 Cadillac Series 62 would be lampooned as a figure of fun.*

By 1956 America owned three-quarters of all the cars in the world. Freeways, multilevel parking lots, shopping centers, drive-ins, and movie theaters sprouted like mushrooms after rain. Americans got high on an orgy of vinyl and power steering.

## Buying into the American Dream

Suddenly stylists replaced designers, and the car shed its machinelike properties to become an instrument of fantasy. Not everyone was enthralled; Woodrow Wilson called the American car "a picture of the arrogance of wealth," and John Keats in his *Insolent Chariots* said "there is little wrong with the American car that is not wrong with the American public."

But Americans were willing, indeed eager, to spend vast amounts each year on a machine that symbolized their desires, reflected themselves, and expressed their fantasies. Detroit made them believe that ever-increasing consumption would genuinely help to build a brighter and richer America.

### PUTTING ON THE RITZ

*The 1953 Packard Caribbean Convertible was one of the most spectacular and lavish cars of the decade. A design that evolved from Packard's recent Pan American show cars, it outsold its arch-rival, the glamorous Cadillac Eldorado.*

And buy they did. In 1955 Detroit shipped eight million new cars to showrooms, accounting for $65 billion or 20 percent of the Gross National Product. GM became the first corporation to earn $1 billion in a single year, and their touring Motorama exhibitions drew two million visitors at every stop. The affluent society rolled effortlessly on, cushioned by fat Goodyear whitewalls. The American car of the Fifties may have been all jets and Jane Russell, but it fanned the flames of the new industrial prosperity, created those rows of neat clapboard houses and those miles of arrow-straight freeways, and gave America an upward mobility that was the envy of the world.

# 1950 CHRYSLER
## *Imperial*

THE IMPERIAL FOUR-DOOR SEDAN COST $3,055 BEFORE OPTIONAL EXTRAS WERE ADDED

IN 1950 CHRYSLER WAS celebrating its silver jubilee, an anniversary year with a sting in its tail. The Office of Price Stabilization had frozen car prices, there was a four-month strike, and serious coal and steel shortages were affecting the industry.

The '50 Imperial was a Chrysler New Yorker with a special roof and interior trim from the Derham Body Company. The jewels in Chrysler's crown, the Imperials were meant to lock horns with the best of Cadillac, Packard, and Lincoln. With Ausco-Lambert disc brakes, Prestomatic transmission, and a MoPar compass, they used the finest technology Chrysler could muster. The trouble was, only 10,650 Imperials drove out of the door in 1950, the hemi-head V8 wouldn't arrive until the next year, buyers were calling it a Chrysler rather than an Imperial, and that frumpy styling looked exactly like what it was – yesterday's lunch warmed up again.

### ENGINE
The inline L-head eight developed 135 bhp and had a cast-iron block with five main bearings. The carburetor was a Carter single-barrel, and Prestomatic automatic transmission with fluid drive came as standard.

### CHRYSLER LOGO
The celebrated designer Virgil Exner joined Chrysler in 1949 but arrived too late to improve the looks of the moribund Imperial.

### INTERIOR
Chryslers interiors were as restrained and conservative as the people who drove them. Turnkey ignition replaced push-button in 1950, which was also the first year of electric windows.

### WINDSHIELD
*The windshield was still old-fashioned two-piece flat glass, which made the Imperial look rather antiquated.*

### REAR WINDOW
*New "Clearbac" rear window used three pieces of glass that were divided by chrome strips.*

### SPECIFICATIONS

MODEL 1950 Chrysler Imperial
PRODUCTION 10,650
BODY STYLE Four-door sedan.
CONSTRUCTION Steel body and chassis.
ENGINE 323cid straight eight.
POWER OUTPUT 135 bhp.
TRANSMISSION Prestomatic semiautomatic.
SUSPENSION *Front:* coil springs; *Rear:* live axle.
BRAKES Front and rear drums, optional front discs.
MAXIMUM SPEED 100 mph (161 km/h)
0–60 MPH (0–96 KM/H) 13 sec
A.F.C. 16 mpg (5.7 km/l)

### BRAKES
*The industry's first disc brakes came as standard on Chrysler Crown Imperials.*

## 1950 CHRYSLER IMPERIAL
Bulky, rounded Chryslers were some of the biggest cars on the road in 1950. The Imperials had Cadillac-style grilles, and the Crown Imperial was a long limousine built to rival the Cadillac 75. In keeping with its establishment image, an Imperial station wagon was never offered. One claim to fame was that MGM Studios used an Imperial-based mobile camera car in many of their film productions.

### SEMIAUTOMATIC TRANSMISSION
The semiautomatic gearbox allowed the driver to use a clutch to pull away, with the automatic taking over as the car accelerated. Imperials had Safety-Level ride, Safety-Rim wheels, Cycle-Bonded brake linings, and a waterproof ignition system.

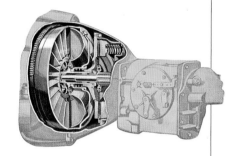

### BRIGHTWORK
*The brightwork on the door sill runs right through between the mudguards. The theme is reflected on the trailing edges of the front grille.*

# 1950 DeSoto
## *Custom*

HERNANDO ADORNS
THE DESOTO LOGO

THE DESOTO OF 1950 had a glittery glamour that cheered up post-war America. Hailed as "cars built for owner satisfaction," they were practical, boxy, and tough. DeSoto was a longtime taxi builder that, in the steel-starved years of 1946–48, managed to turn out 11,600 cabs, most of which plied the streets of New York.

Despite more chrome up front than any other Chrysler product, DeSotos still labored on with an L-head six-cylinder 250cid mill. The legendary Firedome V8 wouldn't arrive until 1952. But body shapes for 1950 were the prettiest ever, and the American public reacted with delight, buying up 133,854 units in the calendar year, ranking DeSoto 14th in the industry. Top-line Custom Convertibles had a very reasonable sticker price of $2,578 and came with Tip-Toe hydraulic shift with Gyrol fluid drive as standard. The austere postwar years were a sales Disneyland for the makers of these sparkling cars, but DeSoto's roll couldn't last. By 1961 it had disappeared forever.

**ADVERTISEMENT**
During the 1950s, car advertising copy became extravagant, relying more on hyperbole than fact. This DeSoto promotion was no exception.

**DeSoto Mascot**
Optional hood ornament was one Hernando DeSoto, a 17th-century Spanish conquistador. The mascot glowed in the dark.

**Rear Wing**
*The DeSoto body shape still carried hints of the separate fenders of prewar cars.*

**Grille**
*The mammoth-tooth grille would be scaled down for 1951. '50 models are easily spotted by their body-color vertical grille divider, unique to this year.*

**INTERIOR**
'50 DeSotos came in two levels of trim. De Luxe, the poverty package, was outsold three to one by the plusher Custom, at $200 more. Direction signals and back-up lights were offered as standard on the Custom, while options included heater, electric clock, and two-tone paint. Convertibles came with whitewalls and wheel covers.

**TRUNK**
*The car's rump was large, round, and unadorned. Trunk space was cavernous.*

**ENGINE**
*All '50 DeSotos shared the same lackluster straight-six engine.*

## 1950 DeSoto Custom Convertible

DeSoto's role at Chrysler was much like Mercury's at Ford and Oldsmobile's at GM, to plug the gap between budget models and uptown swankmobiles. The top-of-the-line Custom range fielded a Club Coupe, two huge wagons, a six-passenger sedan, a two-door Sportsman, and a convertible. DeSoto's volume sellers were its sedans and coupes, which listed at under $2,000 in De Luxe form.

**ENGINE**
The side-valve straight six was stodgy, putting out a modest 112 bhp through the fluid drive gearbox, an innovative semiautomatic pre-selector with conventional manual operation or semiauto kick-down.

### SPECIFICATIONS

**MODEL** 1950 DeSoto Custom Convertible
**PRODUCTION** 2,900
**BODY STYLE** Two-door convertible.
**CONSTRUCTION** Steel body and box-section chassis.
**ENGINE** 236.7cid straight six.
**POWER OUTPUT** 112 bhp.
**TRANSMISSION** Fluid drive semiautomatic.
**SUSPENSION** *Front:* independent coil springs;
*Rear:* leaf springs with live axle.
**BRAKES** Front and rear drums.
**MAXIMUM SPEED** 90 mph (145 km/h)
**0–60 MPH** (0–96 KM/H) 22.1 sec
**A.F.C.** 18 mpg (6.4 km/l)

# 1952 KAISER HENRY J.
## *Corsair*

KAISER LOGO ON THE
STEERING WHEEL

IN THE EARLY 1950s, the major motor manufacturers reckoned that small cars meant small profits, so low-priced transportation was left to independent companies like Nash, Willys, and Kaiser-Frazer. In 1951, a streamlined, Frazerless Kaiser launched "America's Most Important New Car," the Henry J.

An 80 bhp six-cylinder "Supersonic" engine gave the Corsair frugal fuel consumption, with Kaiser claiming that every third mile in a Henry J. was free. The market, however, was unconvinced. At $1,561, the Corsair cost more than the cheapest big Chevy, wasn't built as well, and depreciated rapidly. Small wonder then that only 107,000 were made. Had America's first serious economy car been launched seven years later during the '58 recession, the Henry J. may well have been a best-seller.

### PRODUCTION
The Henry J. was built at the Willow Run factory in Michigan. Despite the caption under the main image that reads "Final inspection. Everything must be perfect," quality was poor, and the car quickly earned itself a second-rate reputation.

### RACING HENRY J.
In 1952, a Henry J. entered the Monte Carlo Rally and, to everybody's surprise, finished in a creditable 20th position.

### CHASSIS
The double-channel box chassis was orthodox and sturdy. The 100 in (2.54 m) wheelbase was short but the interior space generous. America's new family car was "long, low, and handsome. The Henry J. is a joy to drive and comfortable to ride in – the Smart Car for Smart People."

### INTERIOR
The interior was seriously austere and gimmick-free. Apart from overdrive and automatic transmission, very few factory options were available. The few controls included starter, ignition, light, and choke switches.

### REPLACEMENT FENDER
*Bolt-on front and rear fenders were part of the Henry J.'s money-saving philosophy.*

**COLOR SCHEME**
*Blue Satin was one of nine color options available.*

**ROOF LINE**
*High roof line owed its existence to the fact that Kaiser's chairman always wore a hat.*

## SPECIFICATIONS

**MODEL** 1952 Kaiser Henry J. Corsair Deluxe
**PRODUCTION** 12,900
**BODY STYLE** Two-door, five-seater sedan.
**CONSTRUCTION** Steel body and chassis.
**ENGINE** 134cid four, 161cid six.
**POWER OUTPUT** 68–80 bhp.
**TRANSMISSION** Three-speed manual with optional overdrive, optional three-speed Hydra-Matic automatic.
**SUSPENSION** *Front:* coil springs; *Rear:* leaf springs with live axle.
**BRAKES** Front and rear drums.
**MAXIMUM SPEED** 87 mph (140 km/h)
**0–60 MPH** (0–96 KM/H) 17 sec
**A.F.C.** 34 mpg (12 km/l)

## 1952 KAISER HENRY J. CORSAIR DELUXE

The stubborn head of Kaiser industries insisted that the Henry J., originally designed as a full-size car by designer Howard "Dutch" Darrin, be scaled down. American Metal Products of Detroit created the prototype, which Darrin then tweaked, not altogether successfully. Luggage space was among the largest of any passenger sedan; with the rear seat folded there were 50 cu ft of trunk area.

**FIN FASHION**
*Modest dorsal fin was quite fashionable for 1952.*

**BOSS BADGING**
The Henry J. nameplate came from Henry J. Kaiser, chairman of the Kaiser-Frazer Corporation.

**TIRES**
*Corsairs were shod with skinny 5.9x15 tube tires.*

# 1954 CHEVROLET
## *Corvette*

CORVETTE FLAGS FOUND
ON THE CAR'S HOOD

A CARICATURE OF A EUROPEAN roadster, the first Corvette of 1953 was more show than go. With typical flamboyance, Harley Earl was more interested in the way it looked than the way it went. But he did identify that car consumers were growing restless and saw a huge market for a new type of auto opium. With everybody's dreams looking exactly the same, the plastic Vette brought a badly needed shot of designed-in diversity. Early models may have been cramped and slow, but they looked like they'd been lifted straight off a Motorama turntable, which they had. Building them was a nightmare though, and for a while GM lost money on each one. Still, nobody minded because Chevrolet now had a new image – as the company that came up with the first American sports car.

### INTERNAL HANDLES
Like the British sports cars it aped, the '54 Vette's door handles appeared on the inside. Windows were apologetic side curtains that leaked and flapped; it would take two years for glass windows to come into the equation.

### INTERIOR
An aeronautical fantasy, the Corvette's dashboard had a futuristic, space-age feel. Not until 1958 was the row of dials repositioned to a more practical front-of-the-driver location.

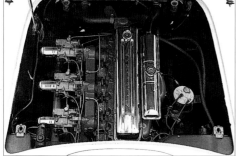

### ENGINE
Souped-up Blue Flame Six may have had triple carbs, higher compression, and a high-lift cam, but it was still old and wheezy. Vettes had to wait until 1955 for the V8 they deserved.

ENGINE WAS MOUNTED
WELL BACK IN FRAME TO
IMPROVE HANDLING

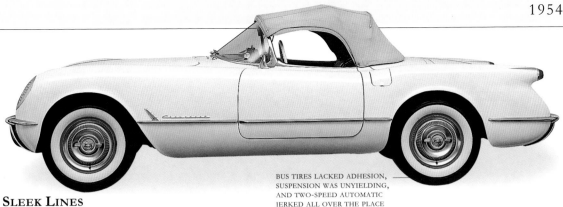

## SLEEK LINES

The cute little body with minimal glitz was one of Earl's best efforts. But, being smitten with jet styling, he couldn't resist adding the "jet pod" taillights, which spoil the car's symmetry.

ODDLY ENOUGH, 80 PERCENT OF ALL '54 CORVETTES WERE PAINTED WHITE

BUS TIRES LACKED ADHESION, SUSPENSION WAS UNYIELDING, AND TWO-SPEED AUTOMATIC JERKED ALL OVER THE PLACE

## OVERVIEW

The cleverly packed fiberglass body was rather tricky to make, with no less than 46 different sections. The convertible top folded out of sight below a neat lift-up panel.

## SPECIFICATIONS

MODEL 1954 Chevrolet Corvette
PRODUCTION 3,640
BODY STYLE Two-door, two-seater sports.
CONSTRUCTION Fiberglass body, steel chassis.
ENGINE 235.5cid straight six.
POWER OUTPUT 150 bhp.
TRANSMISSION Two-speed Powerglide automatic.
SUSPENSION *Front:* coil springs; *Rear:* leaf springs with live axle.
BRAKES Front and rear drums.
MAXIMUM SPEED 107 mph (172 km/h)
0-60 MPH (0-96 KM/H) 8-12 sec
A.F.C. 20 mpg (7 km/l)

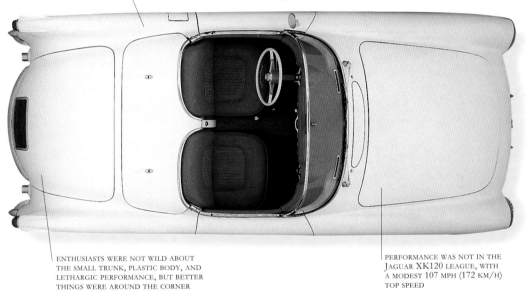

ENTHUSIASTS WERE NOT WILD ABOUT THE SMALL TRUNK, PLASTIC BODY, AND LETHARGIC PERFORMANCE, BUT BETTER THINGS WERE AROUND THE CORNER

PERFORMANCE WAS NOT IN THE JAGUAR XK120 LEAGUE, WITH A MODEST 107 MPH (172 KM/H) TOP SPEED

## EXHIBITION SUCCESS

The Vette's shape was based on the 1952 EX-122 show car, and this was one of the few Motorama dream cars to go into production virtually unchanged. The original plan to produce the Vette in steel was shelved after widespread acclaim for the fiberglass body from visitors to Motorama.

OUTBOARD-MOUNTED REAR LEAF SPRINGS HELPED CORNERING STABILITY

1954 CHEVROLET CORVETTE

# EVOLUTION OF THE CHEVROLET CORVETTE

HOWLING ALONG the freeways of America, the Vette has always been special. In fact, a whole mystique has grown up around Chevy's wild child. Perhaps it's because of its personification of rebellion, no-compromise attitude, or the people that drive them, but the Vette has endured as America's alter ego – proof positive that not everybody wants to pilot slushy barges half-a-block long. When the motoring day of reckoning comes, the Corvette will be up there with the best of them.

## 1953

THAT THE VETTE EXISTS at all is due to the genius of one man – Harley Earl. It started life as no more than a half-formed thought, spinning gently on a Motorama turntable. Within months, the Corvette was a reality and proved the perfect product for a generation of suburban good-timers whose beloved Levis were now feeling the strain.

### KEY FEATURES
• Polo White EX-122 show car wows the crowds at 1952 Motorama
• Production cars have no exterior door handles or side windows
• Base engine is 150 bhp 235.5cid straight six
• Calendar year sales of 300 cars

## 1956

THE V8 LUMP & FUEL injection helped, but that swooping, sculpted body of '56 did more than anything to guarantee the Corvette's future. Macho, sexy, and much more refined, the second-generation Vette ('56–'62) could now lock horns with Uncle Henry's T-Bird – and it had windup windows. Today, it is one of the icons of Fifties car design.

### KEY DEVELOPMENTS
• New 210 bhp 265cid V8 base engine
• New curved body and taillights
• Outside door handles and windup windows instead of clumsy side curtains
• Exhausts exit through rear bumper guards
• Transistorized radio seek option

## 1963

THE STING RAY wowed the world like the Jaguar E-Type. For the first time in the Corvette's history it was a sellout. Demand was up by 50 percent and the factory couldn't cope. Waiting lists stretched to infinity, and nobody got a discount. These were the most desirable Corvettes of all, and that magical '63 split-window Coupe was a car to die for.

### KEY DEVELOPMENTS
• New body and Sting Ray name
• 327cid V8 option
• Improved interior with dual cockpits
• Unique split rear window
• New chassis frame
• Independent rear suspension
• Bigger drum brakes

# 1954 CHEVROLET
## *Corvette*

**REAR PLATE PROBLEMS**
Early cars had license plates in a plastic niche that misted up. Chevrolet inserted two bags of desiccant material to absorb the moisture.

TWIN-COWL DASH WAS PURE BUCK ROGERS

**QUALITY STYLING**
Rear-fender detailing is glorious, and shows Earl's genius at its very best.

IMPACT PROTECTION MAY HAVE BEEN VESTIGIAL, BUT FIBERGLASS BODY TOOK MINOR IMPACT WELL

MN·1744
NY EMPIRE STATE 57

## 1968

CURVY, CHARISMATIC, but compromised, the late '60s Vette was hardly a quantum leap forward. Emasculated by Federal interference and economic, social, and energy neuroses, Chevy was forced to tame its bad boy. Suddenly the Vette changed from a tire-shredding banshee to a blow-dried boulevardier. Ironically, its popularity actually increased.

**KEY DEVELOPMENTS**
- New "Mako Shark" styling
- Redesigned interior
- New T-Top Sport Coupe model with removable roof panels
- Massive 427cid V8 available
- Wipers now behind vacuum-operated panel

## 1978

THE CORVETTE celebrated its silver anniversary in '78, marking the moment with a new fastback roof line and wide rear window that tucked around the car's sides. The interior felt more spacious, and rear vision was vastly improved. A Vette was the official Indy pace car in '78 and Chevy produced a run of 6,200 limited edition look-alikes.

**KEY DEVELOPMENTS**
- Base engine is 350cid V8
- Larger luggage area
- Crossed flags insignia returns to nose and sides
- 500,000th Vette made in 1977
- Optional $995 five-speed gearbox

## 1984

THE ARRIVAL OF the likes of RX-7s, Datsun Zs, and Porsche 928s meant that America's sports car had to grow up fast. The sixth-generation Vette of '83 was the fastest, best-handling, and most radical ever. Engineered from the ground up and truly sophisticated, it was built to take on the world's elite, while still retaining the Corvette's uniquely American personality.

**KEY DEVELOPMENTS**
- Hugely improved roadholding
- Steel backbone chassis with unitized body structure
- New Girlock ventilated disc brakes
- New 4+3 gearbox
- Now one of the half-dozen fastest production cars in the world

## 1992

IN THE WORLD OF THE motor car, 44 years is an eternity for a model name. Yet the Vette has not just survived, it has prospered and become a truly great car. The one-millionth Corvette rolled off the production line in 1992 and, as this book is being written, there's a new Vette poised to steal America's heart all over again.

**KEY DEVELOPMENTS**
- New 300 bhp V8
- ZR-1 option has twin-cam 32-valve with 405 bhp
- LT1 option has six-speed manual or four-speed automatic gearbox
- ABS and driver's-side airbag standard
- GM's first "passive keyless" entry system

---

### EARLY PRODUCTION
The first cars were literally hand built at the Flint, Michigan, factory. Plans to turn out 1,000 cars a month in 1954 were hit by poor early sales.

STONE-GUARDS ON LIGHTS WERE CULLED FROM EUROPEAN RACING CARS, BUT CRITICIZED FOR BEING TOO FEMININE

### GUIDING WORDS
Earl's advice to stylists working on the Corvette was to "go all the way and then back off." They didn't back off much!

EARL ADMITTED THAT SHARK-TOOTH GRILLE WAS ROBBED FROM CONTEMPORARY FERRARIS

MN·1744
NY EMPIRE STATE 57

# 1954 HUDSON
## *Hornet*

BADGE SHOWS TWO
TOWERS AND TWO
GALLEONS

HUDSON DID ITS BEST IN '54 to clean up its aged 1948 body. Smoother flanks and a lower, wider front view helped, along with a new dash and brighter fabrics and vinyls. And at long last the windshield was one piece. Mechanically it wasn't bad either. In fact, some say the last Step-Down was the best ever. With the straight six came a Twin-H power option, a hot camshaft, and an alloy head that could crank out 170 bhp; it was promptly dubbed "The Fabulous Hornet."

The problem was that everybody had V8s, and by mid-1954 Hudson had hemorrhaged over $6 million. In April that year, Hudson, which had been around since 1909, was swallowed up by the Nash-Kelvinator Corporation. Yet the Hornet has been rightly recognized as a milestone car and one of the quickest sixes of the era. If Hudson is to be remembered for anything, it should be for the innovative engineers, who could wring the best from ancient designs and tiny budgets.

**INTERIOR**
The dash was quite modern and glossy but still used Hudson's distinctive single-digit speedo. The Hornet's interior was liberally laced with chrome, and trim was nylon worsted Bedford cloth and Plastihide in brown, blue, or green. Power steering was offered on Hudsons for the first time in '54.

**COLOR CHOICE**
*Hornets came in Roman Bronze, Pasture Green, Algerian Blue, St. Clair Gray, Lipstick Red, or Coronation Cream as here.*

**ENGINE**
*Amazingly, Hudson never offered V8 power, which was to hasten its downfall.*

**TRIM**
*Extra chrome trim was new for '54.*

### LIGHTS
*These cowled single headlights would be replaced by quad lights in '58.*

### FLOORING
*Wood-bed floors helped to protect the load area and added a quality feel.*

### ENGINE
*The small-block V8 produced 150 bhp and could cruise at 70 mph (113 km/h).*

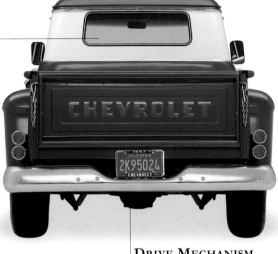

### REAR WINDOW
*De Luxe models had a larger, wrap-around windshield.*

## 1957 CHEVROLET 3100 STEPSIDE
Chevy's '57 pickups can be identified by the new trapezoid grille and a flatter hood than '56 models. Buyers had a choice of short or long pickup, De Luxe or standard trim, and 11 exterior colors. Engines were the 235cid Thriftmaster six or the 265cid Trademaster V8.

### SPECIFICATIONS
MODEL  1957 Chevrolet 3100 Stepside
PRODUCTION  Not available
BODY STYLE  Two-seater, short-bed pickup.
CONSTRUCTION  Steel body and chassis.
ENGINE  235cid six, 265cid V8.
POWER OUTPUT  130–145 bhp.
TRANSMISSION  Three-speed manual with overdrive, optional three-speed automatic.
SUSPENSION  *Front:* coil springs; *Rear:* leaf springs.
BRAKES  Front and rear drums.
MAXIMUM SPEED  80 mph (129 km/h)
0–60 MPH (0–96 KM/H)  17.3 sec
A.F.C.  17 mpg (6 km/l)

### DRIVE MECHANISM
*From '55 on, all Chevys used open-drive instead of an enclosed torque-tube driveline.*

### STEP
*This neat rear step allows access to the load area and gives the pickup its Stepside name.*

# 1957 CHRYSLER
## *New Yorker*

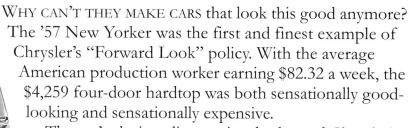

THE 1957 NEW YORKER
CONVERTIBLE COUPE

WHY CAN'T THEY MAKE CARS that look this good anymore? The '57 New Yorker was the first and finest example of Chrysler's "Forward Look" policy. With the average American production worker earning $82.32 a week, the $4,259 four-door hardtop was both sensationally good-looking and sensationally expensive.

The car's glorious lines seriously alarmed Chrysler's competitors, especially since the styling was awarded two gold medals, the suspension was by newfangled torsion bar, and muscle was courtesy of one of the most respected engines in the world – the hemi-head Fire Power, which in the New Yorker cranked out 325 horses. Despite this, "the most glamorous cars of a generation" cost Chrysler a whopping $300 million and sales were disappointing. One of the problems was a propensity for rust, along with shabby fit and finish; another was low productivity – only a measly 10,948 four-door hardtop models rolled out of the Highland Park factory. Even so, the New Yorker was certainly one of the most beautiful cars Chrysler ever made.

### INTERIOR
New Yorkers had it all. Equipment included power windows, a six-way power seat, Hi-Way Hi-Fi phonograph, Electro-Touch radio, rear seat speaker, Instant Air heater, handbrake warning system, Air-Temp air-conditioning, and tinted glass – an altogether impressive array of features for a 1957 automobile.

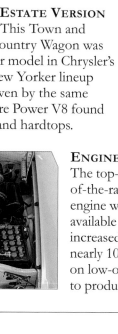

### SUBTLE STYLING
*The New Yorker has few styling excesses. Even the seven gratuitous slashes on the rear fender do not look over the top.*

### ESTATE VERSION
This Town and Country Wagon was another model in Chrysler's 1957 New Yorker lineup and was driven by the same impressive Fire Power V8 found in the sedan and hardtops.

### ENGINE
The top-of-the-range model had a top-of-the-range motor. The hemi-head engine was the largest production plant available in 1957. Bore and stroke were increased and displacement raised by nearly 10 percent. It was efficient, ran on low-octane gas, and could be tickled to produce staggering outputs.

## 1957 CHRYSLER NEW YORKER

Chrysler stunned the world with its dartlike shapes of 1957. The unified design was created by the mind of one man – Virgil Exner – rather than by a committee, and it shows. Those prodigious rear fenders sweep up gracefully, harmonizing well with the gently tapering roof line. The low belt line, huge expanse of glass, and slinky profile are commendably subtle.

**TIRES**
*Optional Captive-Aire tires were available, with promises that they wouldn't let themselves down.*

**REAR VIEW**
*Rather than looking overstyled, the rear end and deck are actually quite restrained. The license plate sits neatly in its niche, the tail pipes are completely concealed, the bumper is understated, and even the rear lights are not too heavy-handed.*

PENNSYLVANIA
**DSK 148**
57 CHRYSLER

### SPECIFICATIONS

MODEL 1957 Chrysler New Yorker
PRODUCTION 34,620
 (all body styles)
BODY STYLE Four-door,
 six-seater hardtop.
CONSTRUCTION Monocoque.
ENGINE 392cid V8.
POWER OUTPUT 325 bhp.
TRANSMISSION Three-speed
 TorqueFlite automatic.
SUSPENSION *Front:* A-arms and
 longitudinal torsion bar;
 *Rear:* semi-elliptic leaf springs.
BRAKES Front and rear drums.
MAXIMUM SPEED 115 mph
 (185 km/h)
0–60 MPH (0–96 KM/H) 12.3 sec
A.F.C. 13 mpg (4.6 km/l)

# 1958 BUICK
## *Limited Riviera*

1942 LIMITED BADGE,
USED AGAIN IN 1958

WHEN YOUR FORTUNES are flagging, you pour on the chrome. As blubbery barges go, the '58 Limited has to be one of the gaudiest. Spanning 19 ft (5.78 m) and tipping the scales at two tons, the Limited is empirical proof that 1958 was not Buick's happiest year. Despite all that twinkling kitsch and the reincarnated Limited badge, the bulbous Buick bombed. For a start, GM's Dynaflow transmission was not up to Hydra-Matic standards, and the brakes were not always trustworthy. Furthermore, in what was a recession year for the industry, the Limited had been priced into Cadillac territory – $33 more than the Series 62. Total production for the Limited in 1958 was a very limited 7,436 units. By the late Fifties, Detroit had lost its way, and the '58 Limited was on the road to nowhere.

FENDER
ORNAMENTS
MAY LOOK
ABSURD BUT
WERE USEFUL
IN PARKING
THE BUICK'S
HUGE GIRTH

### ENGINE
The Valve-in-Head B12000 engine kicked out 300 horses, with a 364 cubic inch displacement. These specifications were respectable enough on paper, but on the road the Limited was too heavy to be anything other than sluggish.

## CHROME CRAZY

THE 1950S WAS THE DECADE OF consumerism. A confident post-war America saw manufacturers developing new products each year, producing goods with limited lifespans and creating a "fad culture"; new materials were being developed and marketed to a "must have" public. Chromium was one example. The metal with a shiny coating swept the nation and, apart from adorning cars and motorcycles, could be found on the surfaces of products as diverse as food mixers and radios, refrigerators and wall clocks. It really was the ultimate, all-purpose, star-spangled metal.

A CHROME
FOOD MIXER
FROM THE
1950S

CHROME
KITCHEN
FURNITURE
WAS ALL THE
RAGE IN THE
FIFTIES

## REAR DESIGN

*The Buick's butt was a confused jumble of bosomy curves, slanting fins, and horizontal flashings. The trunk itself was big enough to house a football team.*

## WINDSHIELD

*The large windshield was served by wide-angle wipers and an automatic windshield washer.*

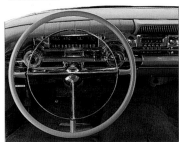

## SPECIFICATIONS

**MODEL** 1958 Buick Limited Riviera Series 700
**PRODUCTION** 7,436 (all body styles)
**BODY STYLE** Two- and four-door, six-seater hardtops, two-door convertible.
**CONSTRUCTION** Steel monocoque.
**ENGINE** 364cid V8.
**POWER OUTPUT** 300 bhp.
**TRANSMISSION** Flight-Pitch Dynaflow automatic.
**SUSPENSION** *Front:* coil springs with A-arms; *Rear:* live axle with coil springs. Optional air suspension.
**BRAKES** Front and rear drums.
**MAXIMUM SPEED** 110 mph (177 km/h)
**0–60 MPH (0–96 KM/H)** 9.5 sec
**A.F.C.** 13 mpg (4.6 km/l)

## 1958 BUICK LIMITED RIVIERA

Buick's answer to an aircraft carrier was a riot of ornamentation that went on for half a block. At rest, the Limited looked like it needed a fifth wheel to support that weighty rear overhang. Air-Poise suspension was an extra-cost option that used pressurized air bladders for a supposedly smooth hydraulic ride. The system was, however, a nightmare to service and literally let itself down.

## TRIMMINGS

*Interiors were trimmed in gray cloth and vinyl or Cordaveen. Seat cushions had Double-Depth foam rubber.*

## GRILLE

*The "Fashion-Aire Dynastar" grille consisted of no fewer than 160 chrome squares, each with four polished facets to give some serious sparkle.*

## INTERIOR

Power steering and brakes were essential and came as standard. Other standard equipment included an electric clock, cigarette lighters, and electric windows.

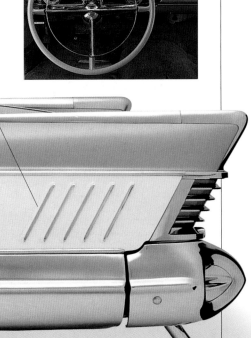

## DECORATION

*Unique to the Limited were 15 utterly pointless chrome slashes down both rear fenders.*

# 1958 EDSEL
## *Bermuda*

TRANSPORTATION FOR THE LARGEST OF FAMILIES

**EDSEL MASCOT**
The Edsel name was chosen from 6,000 possibilities, including Mongoose, Turcotinga, and Utopian Turtletop.

WITHOUT THAT INFAMOUS GRILLE, the Bermuda wouldn't have been a bad old barge. The rest looked pretty safe and suburban, and even those faddish rear lights weren't that offensive. At $3,155 it was the top Edsel wagon, wooing the public with more mock wood than Disneyland. But Ford had oversold the Edsel big time, and every model suffered guilt by association. Initial sales in 1957 were nothing like the predicted 200,000 but weren't disastrous either. The Bermudas, though, found just 2,235 buyers and were discontinued after only one year. By 1958, people no longer believed the hype, and Edsel sales evaporated; the company ceased trading in November 1959. Everybody knew that the '58 recession killed the Edsel, but at Ford major players in the project were cruelly demoted or fired

**INTERIOR**
Never one of Edsel's strongest selling points, the Teletouch gear selector was operated by push buttons on the steering wheel. It was gimmicky and unreliable.

TELETOUCH BUTTON SENT A SIGNAL TO THE CAR'S "PRECISION BRAIN"

E400 ON VALVE COVERS INDICATES AMOUNT OF TORQUE

**ENGINE**
"They're the industry's newest – and the best," cried the advertising. Edsel engines were strong 361 or 410cid V8s, with the station wagons usually powered by the smaller unit.

**FORD WHEELBASE**
*Edsel wagons were based on the 116 in (295 cm) Ford station wagon platform.*

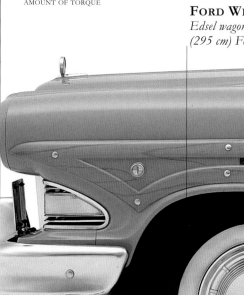

## 1958 EDSEL BERMUDA

Looking back, one wonders how one of the most powerful corporations in the world could possibly have signed off on such a stylistic debacle. '58 Edsels weren't just ugly, they were appallingly weird. The Bermuda's side view is innocuous enough and no worse than many half-timbered shopping center wagons of the period. Note how the roof is slightly kinked to give the huge panel extra rigidity.

## SPECIFICATIONS

**MODEL** 1958 Edsel Bermuda
**PRODUCTION** 1,456 (six-seater Bermudas)
**BODY STYLE** Four-door, six-seater station wagon.
**CONSTRUCTION** Steel body and chassis.
**ENGINE** 361cid V8.
**POWER OUTPUT** 303 bhp.
**TRANSMISSION** Three-speed manual with optional overdrive, optional three-speed automatic with or without Teletouch control.
**SUSPENSION** *Front:* independent coil springs; *Rear:* leaf springs with live axle.
**BRAKES** Front and rear drums.
**MAXIMUM SPEED** 108 mph (174 km/h)
**0–60 MPH (0–96 KM/H)** 10.2 sec
**A.F.C.** 15 mpg (5.3 km/l)

**FRONT VIEW**
*Grille was so prominent that it required separate flanking bumpers.*

**LIGHTS**
*Zany boomerang rear clusters contained turn signal, stop, and reverse lights.*

**INTERIOR**
*All wagons had four armrests, two coathooks, dome lights, and vinyl white headlining.*

**COLOR**
*This Bermuda is painted in Spring Green, but buyers had a choice of 161 different color combinations.*

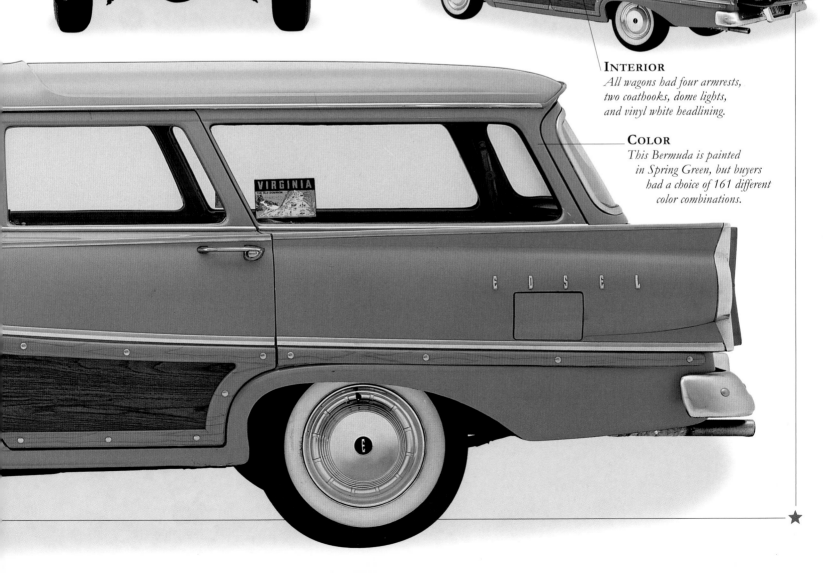

# 1958 LINCOLN
## *Capri*

A RANGE OF ALL-NEW LINCOLNS WERE BROUGHT
OUT IN 1958 TO CHALLENGE CADILLAC

IN POSSIBLY ONE OF the most outrageous half-truths ever written, Lincoln copywriters insisted that the '58 Capri was "impressive without being ostentatious" and had a "tasteful, classic elegance." In reality, it was a stylistic nightmare, two-and-a-half tons of massive bumpers, sculpted wheel arches, and weirdly canted headlights. What's more, in the jumbo 430cid Continental V8 it had the largest engine available in an American production car at the time.

This visual anarchy and the '58 recession meant that sales halved from the previous year, and Ford realized that the Capri was as badly timed as the Edsel. Even so, the luxury Lincoln had one solid advantage: it was quick *and* it handled. One magazine said, "it's doubtful if any big car could stick any tighter in the corners or handle any better at high speed," a homily helped by the unitary body, rear coil springs, and potent new brakes. The '58 Capri was one of the last driveaway dinosaurs. The door was closing on an era of kitsch.

### UNITARY BODY
In '58, Lincoln switched to a unitary body, eliminating a chassis frame for the first time in 10 years. Suspension, drivetrain, and engine units were fastened to the body structure to minimize weight and offer a smoother ride. However, prototypes flexed so badly that all sorts of stiffening reinforcements were added, negating any weight savings.

### STYLING
*The Capri used every stylistic trick that Motown had ever learned, but only desperate men would put fins on the rear bumper.*

### ENGINE
The big new 430cid V8 engine walloped out 375 horses, giving a power output second only to the Chrysler 300D. Lowered final drive ratios failed even to pay lipservice to fuel economy, with the Capri returning a groan-inspiring 10 mpg (3.5 km/l) around town.

### INTERIOR
For a price just short of $5,000, standard features included electric windows with childproof controls, a six-way Power Seat, a padded instrument panel, and five ashtrays, each with its own lighter. Seat belts and leather trim were optional.

**SUSPENSION**
*This was the first year that Lincolns had coil springs for rear suspension.*

# 1958 LINCOLN CAPRI

Lincoln's dramatic restyle of '58 was not one of their happiest. The frivolous fins of '57 were trimmed down, but the sculpted bumpers and scalloped fenders were still a mess. Ford's brief for the '58 Lincolns was to out-glitz Cadillac in every area, but somehow they didn't quite get it right. Instead, the Lincoln made the Caddy Eldorado look downright divine.

**INTERIOR**
*The largest passenger car of the year, the Capri could accommodate six or even seven people, riding on an enormous, elongated 131 in (3.33 m) wheelbase.*

**FINS**
*By '58 the size of fins was falling, partly due to fashion, and also to reduce the risk of injuring pedestrians in road accidents.*

**WINDSCREEN**
*Tinted glass was a $50 option, along with translucent sun visors at $27.*

## SPECIFICATIONS

**MODEL** 1958 Lincoln Capri
**PRODUCTION** 6,859
**BODY STYLE** Four-door, six-seater sedan.
**CONSTRUCTION** Steel unitary body.
**ENGINE** 430cid V8.
**POWER OUTPUT** 375 bhp.
**TRANSMISSION** Three-speed Turbodrive automatic.
**SUSPENSION** Front and rear coil springs.
**BRAKES** Front and rear drums.
**MAXIMUM SPEED** 115 mph (185 km/h)
**0–60 MPH** (0–96 KM/H) 9 sec
**A.F.C.** 14 mpg (5 km/l)

**TIRE SIZE**
*9x14 tires couldn't cope with the Lincoln's prodigious weight. Cost-cutting and an obsession with a soft ride meant that most cars of the period wallowed around on potentially lethal undersized rubber.*

PA '58
H19·912

# 1958 PACKARD
## *Hawk*

SALES LITERATURE HERALDED THE
ARRIVAL OF "A DISTINCTIVE, NEW,
FULL-POWERED SPORTS-STYLED CAR"

DISTINCTIVE, BIZARRE, AND VERY un-American, the '58 Hawk was a pastiche of European styling cues. Which is why there were no quad headlights, no athletic profile, and no glinting chromium dentures on the grille. Inspired by the likes of Ferrari and Mercedes, it boasted tan pleated-leather hide, white-on-black instruments, Jaguaresque fender vents, a turned metal dashboard, gulping hood air-scoop, and a broad fiberglass shovel-nostril that could have been lifted off a Maserati. And it was supercharged.

But Packard's desperate attempt to distance itself from traditional Detroit iron failed. At $4,000, the Hawk was overpriced, underrefined, and overdecorated. Packard had merged with Studebaker back in 1954, and although it was initially a successful alliance, problems with suppliers and another buyout in 1956 basically sealed the company's fate. Only 588 Hawks were built, with the very last Packard rolling off the South Bend, Indiana, line on July 13, 1958. Today the Hawk stands as a quaint curiosity, a last-ditch attempt to preserve the Packard pedigree. It remains one of the most fiercely desired of the final Packards.

**EURO STYLING**
The door mirror was designed to replicate the knock-off hub spinners of wire wheels on European sports cars, but it looked out of place with the Hawk's discreet styling.

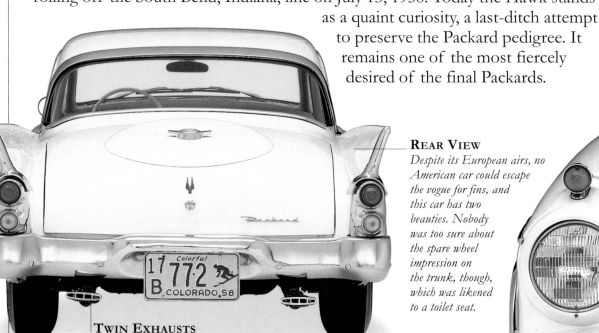

**REAR VIEW**
*Despite its European airs, no American car could escape the vogue for fins, and this car has two beauties. Nobody was too sure about the spare wheel impression on the trunk, though, which was likened to a toilet seat.*

**TWIN EXHAUSTS**
*Standard on the Hawk, but fishtail embellishers were an optional accessory.*

**ENGINE**
Flight-O-Matic automatic transmission and a hefty, supercharged 289cid V8 came standard, hurling out 275 horses; 0–60 mph (96 km/h) took just under eight seconds. The Hawk's blower was a belt-driven McCulloch supercharger.

"SUPERCHARGED "GO" AT THE TIP OF YOUR TOE," READ THE BROCHURE

### AIR VENTS
*Front fender vents were shamelessly culled from British Mark IX and XK Jaguars.*

### 1958 PACKARD HAWK
Uniquely, the Hawk had exterior vinyl armrests running along the side windows and a refreshing lack of chrome gaudiness on the flanks. The roof line and halo roof band are aeronautical, the belt line is tense and urgent, and the whole plot stood on 14-inch wheels to make it look lower and meaner.

### STEERING
*Power steering was a $70 factory option.*

### FRONT ASPECT
*The Hawk was one of the few Packards that dared to sport single headlights and, along with that softly shaped front bumper and mailbox air intake, looked nothing like contemporary Americana.*

### SPECIFICATIONS

**MODEL** 1958 Packard Hawk
**PRODUCTION** 588
**BODY STYLE** Two-door, four-seater coupe.
**CONSTRUCTION** Steel body and chassis.
**ENGINE** 289cid V8.
**POWER OUTPUT** 275 bhp.
**TRANSMISSION** Three-speed Flight-O-Matic automatic, optional overdrive.
**SUSPENSION** *Front:* independent coil springs; *Rear:* leaf springs.
**BRAKES** Front and rear drums.
**MAXIMUM SPEED** 125 mph (201 km/h)
**0–60 MPH (0–96 KM/H)** 8 sec
**A.F.C.** 15 mpg (5.3 km/l)

### INTERIOR
To stress the Hawk's supposed sporting bloodline, the interior was clad in soft hide with sports-car instrumentation. In addition, you could specify a raft of convenience options that included power windows and air-conditioning.

# 1958 RAMBLER
## *Ambassador*

THIS IS A
DOUBLE–SAFE
**SINGLE UNIT
BODY**
BUILT WITH AN ADVANCED METHOD OF BODY CONSTRUCTION IN WHICH THE BODY AND FRAME ARE COMBINED INTO A SINGLE ALL-WELDED STRUCTURAL UNIT
PIONEERED AND BUILT EXCLUSIVELY BY
**AMERICAN MOTORS CORP.**
DETROIT        MICHIGAN

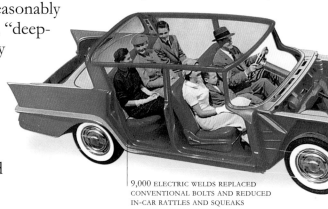

WHILE THE GOVERNMENT WAS telling consumers "You auto buy now," American Motors boss George Romney was telling the President that "Consumers are rebelling against the size, horsepower, and excessive styling of the American automobile."

Romney's Ramblers were the only industry success story for a recession-racked 1958 when, for the first time ever, more cars were imported than exported. The Ambassador was Rambler's economy flagship, and road testers liked the speed, room, luxury, thrift, and high resale value. Also, it was reasonably priced, had a safety package option, "deep-dip" rustproofing, and a thoroughly modern monocoque shell. But buyers weren't buying. Motorists may have wanted economy and engineering integrity, but cars still had to be cool. The sensible Ambassador was an ugly, slab-sided machine for middle-aged squares.

SALES LITERATURE PLUGGED THE 1958 AMBASSADOR'S SUPERIOR ECONOMY AND HANDLING

9,000 ELECTRIC WELDS REPLACED CONVENTIONAL BOLTS AND REDUCED IN-CAR RATTLES AND SQUEAKS

### WHAT, NO CHASSIS?
Chassis-less body construction was a Nash/AMC tradition also used by many European nameplates, namely Jaguar. Few American manufacturers were interested in following suit. Despite modest dimensions, the Ambassador was accommodating; it had a very high roof line and could just about carry six passengers.

### INTERIOR
The custom steering wheel was an option, along with power steering at $89.50. Flash-O-Matic automatic transmission could be column-operated or controlled by push buttons on the dashboard. The Weather-Eye heater, another option, was thought to be one of the most efficient in the industry.

## 1958 RAMBLER AMBASSADOR

AMC stylist Ed Anderson did a good job with the '58 models, cleverly reskinning '56 and '57s with longer hoods, different grilles, and taillights. But with modest tail fins and a plain rump, the Ambassador was no matinee idol and looked more like a taxi than an upscale sedan. The six cars in the range included three station wagons.

### ENGINE

The cast-iron 327cid V8 motor gave 270 bhp and, despite a one-barrel carb, could reach 60 mph (96 km/h) in 10 seconds. The same engine had powered the '57 Rambler Rebel.

### SPECIFICATIONS

**MODEL** 1958 Rambler Ambassador
**PRODUCTION** 14,570 (all body styles)
**BODY STYLE** Four-door, six-seater sedan.
**CONSTRUCTION** Steel monocoque body.
**ENGINE** 327cid V8.
**POWER OUTPUT** 270 bhp.
**TRANSMISSION** Three-speed manual with optional overdrive, optional three-speed Flash-O-Matic automatic.
**SUSPENSION** *Front:* independent coil springs; *Rear:* coil with optional air springs.
**BRAKES** Front and rear drums.
**MAXIMUM SPEED** 105 mph (169 km/h)
**0–60 MPH (0–96 KM/H)** 10 sec
**A.F.C.** 18 mpg (6.4 km/l)

### MODEST FINS

*Sales literature championed the "sensible fin height" as an aid to safer driving by not obstructing rear vision.*

### SUSPENSION

*Rear air suspension was an optional extra, but few buyers ordered it. Just as well, because reliability problems caused the industry to drop the whole concept soon after.*

### ORNAMENTATION

*The sweepspear was one of the Ambassador's few concessions to ornamentation, and helped to break up an otherwise solid flank.*

# 1959 CADILLAC
## *Eldorado*

THE '59 CADILLAC ISN'T SO MUCH a car as a cathedral– a gothic monument to America's glory years. Overlong, overlow, and overstyled, it stands as the final flourish of the Fifties. We might marvel at its way-out space-age styling, those bizarre fins, and that profligate 390 cubic inch V8, but the most telling thing about the '59 is its sheer in-yer-face arrogance.

STAMP CELEBRATES THE CADILLAC'S MOST OUTSTANDING FEATURE

Back in the Fifties, the United States was the most powerful nation on earth. With money to burn, military might, arrow-straight freeways, and Marilyn Monroe, America really thought it could reach out and touch the Moon. But when the '59 Caddy appeared, that nationalistic high was ebbing away. The Russians had launched Sputnik, Castro was getting chummy with Khrushchev, and there were race riots at home. A decade of glitz, glamour, and prosperity was coming to an end. America would never be the same again, and neither would her Cadillacs.

### ENGINE
Base engine on the '59 was a five-bearing 390cid V8 with hydraulic lifters and high compression heads. Breathing through a Carter four-barrel, it developed 325 bhp, but with the Eldorado V8 and three Rochester two-barrels the '59 could muster an extra 20 bhp.

### INTERIOR
Standard lavish fare on the '59 Convertible – power brakes, power steering, auto transmission, power windows, two-speed windshield wipers, and a two-way power seat.

### CADILLAC COUPE DE VILLE
The de Ville lineup was two sedans and a coupe, trimmed like the Series 6200 with the same standards plus electric windows and power seats. Sticker prices were $5,498 (Sedan) and $5,252 (Coupe).

### AUTRONIC EYE
Automatic headlight-dipping came courtesy of the optional Autronic Eye, which could sense the lights of oncoming cars. At just $55, futuristic technology had never been so accessible.

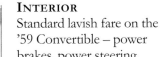

### UP-TO-DATE FEATURES
*Options were amazingly modern, with air suspension, cruise control, remote trunk lock, and bucket seats.*

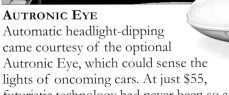

to draw blood. Satirists laid into the fin with vicious glee. John Keats, in his book *The Insolent Chariots*, likened the American car to an overweight concubine. "With all the subtlety of a madam affecting a lorgnette, she put tail fins on her overblown bustle and spouted wavering antennae from each fin."

BELIEVE IT OR NOT, THE FINS ON THE '60 CHEVY IMPALA WERE ACTUALLY TONED DOWN FROM '59

Surprisingly, Virgil Exner, Chrysler's design guru, bravely attempted to argue that fins had a practical advantage. Using a scale model of a DeSoto in a wind tunnel, he claimed that roadholding was improved and steering corrections in strong crosswinds reduced by up to 20 percent. But in reality it was impossible to argue with conviction that this absurd stylistic excess had a serious function. After fins had shrunk in the early Sixties, no one reported worse handling or steering vagaries.

The fin was really the first of a cornucopia of visual novelties that gave consumers a reason for changing their cars every year. Cynically, the industry knew that these appalling appendages were just a tool to hasten the process of dynamic obsolescence, but a gullible public identified the fin with luxury and prestige, taking it as the punctuation mark of a well-styled car. It is endlessly fascinating to think that such a simple styling device managed so completely to entrance an entire decade of American car buyers.

THE EXPERIMENTAL CADILLAC CYCLONE TOOK THE FIN MOTIF TO NEW EXTREMES

### FADDISH FRONT

The front end was the auto industry's idea of high style in '59. Quad headlights had ridiculous hooded chrome eyebrows, and the grille was outrageously overwrought. Such ostentation was merely a crutch for hobbling from one expensive restyle to the next.

WINDSHIELD IS SOLEX TINTED, AN $18 OPTIONAL EXTRA

VARIABLE-SPEED WINDSHIELD WIPERS AND WASHERS COST $18.25 EXTRA BACK IN '59

THE ABSURD OVER-CHROMED OVERRIDERS HOLD PARKING LIGHTS

R·2885

NY EMPIRE STATE 60

# 1959 EDSEL
## *Corsair*

STEERING WHEEL LOGO

BY 1959 AMERICA HAD LOST her confidence; the economy nose-dived, Russia was first in space, there were race riots in Little Rock, and Ford was counting the cost of its disastrous Edsel project – close to 400 million dollars. "The Edsel look is here to stay" brayed the ads, but the bold new vertical grille had become a country-wide joke. Sales didn't just die, they never took off, and those who had been rash enough to buy hid their chromium follies in suburban garages. Eisenhower's mantra of materialism was over, and buyers wanted to know more about economical compacts like the Nash Rambler, Studebaker Lark, and novel VW Beetle. Throw in a confusing 18-model line-up, poor build quality, and disenchanted dealers, and "The Newest Thing on Wheels" never stood a chance. Now famous as a powerful symbol of failure, the Edsel stands as a sad memorial to the foolishness of consumer culture in Fifties America.

### — EDSEL HYPE —

FORD HAD CANVASSED public opinion on a new design with which to challenge GM's dominance as far back as 1954, and named the new project the E ("experimental") Car. Officially christened the Edsel, it arrived in 1957 on the back of intense TV and magazine coverage. But by the time it hit the showrooms, the market had done an about-face and wanted more than just empty chromium rhetoric. The main problem was that the Edsel's vision was never taken beyond yesterday or today. No input into the project considered the future, so by the time the Edsel did appear, it was a ridiculous leviathan, hopelessly out of kilter with its time.

**REAR LIGHTS**
*Tail and backup lights were shared with the '58 Continental to save on tooling costs.*

**1959 EDSEL CORSAIR CONVERTIBLE**
By 1959, the Corsair had become just a restyled Ranger, based on the Ford Fairlane. Corsairs had bigger motors and more standard equipment. But even a sticker price of $3,000 for the convertible didn't help sales, which were a miserable model year total of 45,000. Ford was desperate and tried to sell it as "A new kind of car that makes sense."

**DECORATION**
*The dominating chrome and white sweepspear that runs the entire length of the car makes the rear deck look heavy.*

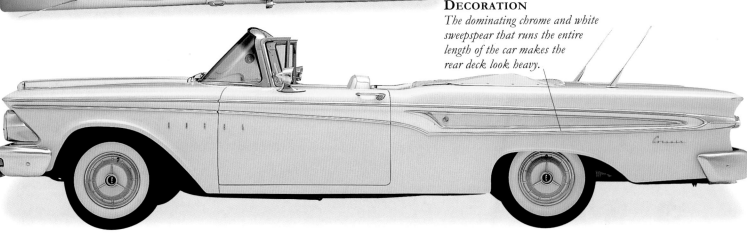

### INTERIOR
The dashboard was cleaned up for 1959, and the unreliable Teletouch transmission deleted in favor of a Mile-O-Matic two-speed with column shift. The eight-tube push-button radio was available at $64.95.

### IN-CAR VINYL
This charming Philips record player is an optional accessory fitted in the early 1960s.

### MIRROR
The hooded chrome door mirror was remote-controlled, an extremely rare option.

"GUARD RAIL" FRAME DESIGN WITH FULL-LENGTH SIDE RAILS

BALL JOINT FRONT SUSPENSION

### CHASSIS
The substantial steel girder chassis incorporated full-length side rails and five cross-members. It was hauled along by either an Edsel Express 332cid V8 producing 225 bhp or a Super Express 361cid V8 developing 303 bhp. 77 percent of all 1959 Edsels were powered by V8s, with the Economy Six making up the numbers.

### SPECIFICATIONS

**MODEL** 1959 Edsel Corsair Convertible
**PRODUCTION** 1,343
**BODY STYLE** Two-door, five-seater convertible.
**CONSTRUCTION** Steel body and chassis.
**ENGINE** 332cid, 361cid V8s.
**POWER OUTPUT** 225–303 bhp.
**TRANSMISSION** Three-speed manual with optional overdrive, optional two- or three-speed Mile-O-Matic automatic.
**SUSPENSION** *Front:* independent with coil springs; *Rear:* leaf springs with live axle.
**BRAKES** Front and rear drums.
**MAXIMUM SPEED** 95–105 mph (153–169 km/h)
**0–60 MPH (0–96 KM/H)** 11–16 sec
**A.F.C.** 15 mpg (5.3 km/l)

### FRONT VIEW
*Roy Brown, the Edsel's designer, claimed that "The front theme of our newest car combines nostalgia with modern vertical thrust." Other pundits compared it to a horse collar, a man sucking a lemon, or even a toilet seat.*

### COLOR
*Petal Yellow was one of 17 possible exterior colors.*

# 1959 FORD
## *Fairlane 500 Skyliner*

THE '59 SKYLINER WAS 3 IN (7½ CM)
SHORTER THAN THE '57–'58 MODELS

FORD RAISED THE ROOF in '57 with its glitziest range ever, and the "Retrac" was a party piece. The world's only mass-produced retractable hardtop debuted at the New York Show of '56, and the first production version was presented to a bemused President Eisenhower in '57. The Skyliner's balletic routine was the most talked-about gadget for years and filled Ford showrooms with thousands of gawking customers.

Surprisingly reliable and actuated by a single switch, the Retrac's roof had 610 ft (185 m) of wiring, three drive motors, and a feast of electrical hardware. But showmanship apart, the Skyliner was pricey and had precious little trunk space or leg room. By '59 the novelty had worn off, and division chief Robert McNamara's desire to end expensive "gimmick engineering" led to the wackiest car ever to come out of Dearborn being axed in 1960.

### ROOF SEQUENCE
A switch on the steering column started three motors that opened the rear deck. Another motor unlocked the top, and yet another motor hoisted the roof and sent it back to the open trunk space. A separate mechanism then lowered the rear deck back into place. It all took just one minute but had to be done with the gear shift in "Park" and the engine running.

### ENGINE
*The Skyliner's standard power was a 292cid V8, but this model contains the top-spec Thunderbird 352cid Special V8 with 300 bhp.*

### REAR STYLING

*Fins were down for '59, but missile-shaped pressings on the higher rear fenders were a neat touch to hide all that moving metalwork.*

### 1959 FORD FAIRLANE 500 GALAXIE SKYLINER RETRACTABLE

The Skyliner lived for three years but was never a volume seller. Buyers may have thought it neat, but they were justifiably anxious about the roof mechanism's reliability. Just under 21,000 were sold in '57, less than 15,000 in '58, and a miserly 12,915 found buyers in '59. At two tons and $3,138, it was the heaviest, priciest, and least practical Ford in the range.

### MANUAL OPERATION

*If the power failed, there was a manual procedure for getting the roof down, but it was rarely needed.*

### FUEL TANK

*This was located behind the rear seat, not for safety but because there was nowhere else to put it.*

### INTERIOR

Available options included power windows, tinted glass, a four-way power seat, and Polar-Aire air-conditioning. The $19 Lifeguard safety package included a padded instrument panel and sun visor.

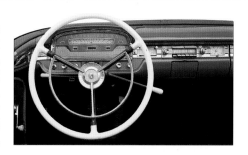

The new
**FORD
SKYLINER**

world's only
**Hide-Away
Hardtop**

### SKYLINER COSTS

Ford spent $18 million testing the Skyliner's roof. Ironically, the Retrac's biggest fault wasn't electrical problems but body rust.

### — SPECIFICATIONS —

**MODEL** 1959 Ford Fairlane 500 Galaxie Skyliner Retractable

**PRODUCTION** 12,915

**BODY STYLE** Two-door hardtop with retractable roof.

**CONSTRUCTION** Steel body and chassis.

**ENGINE** 272cid, 292cid, 312cid, 352cid V8s.

**POWER OUTPUT** 190–300 bhp.

**TRANSMISSION** Three-speed manual, optional three-speed Cruise-O-Matic automatic.

**SUSPENSION** *Front:* coil springs; *Rear:* leaf springs.

**BRAKES** Front and rear drums.

**MAXIMUM SPEED** 105 mph (169 km/h)

**0–60 MPH (0–96 KM/H)** 10.6 sec

**A.F.C.** 15.3 mpg (5.4 km/l)

# 1959 PLYMOUTH
## *Fury*

*Fury*

A BOLD AND BRASSY NAME FOR
PLYMOUTH'S KITSCH CLASSIC

AMAZINGLY, THE '59 FURY was aimed squarely at middle-class, middle-income America. Amazingly, because it was as loud as Little Richard and as sexy as Jayne Mansfield. One of the most stylistically adventurous cars on the road, the futuristic Fury was pure "Forward Look." Plymouth's ads bellowed that it was "three full years" ahead of its time, and the '59 model was the most strident of the lot. That razor-edged profile made Plymouth a nameplate to kill for, especially if it was the top-of-the-line Sport Fury, which came with a personalized aluminum plaque that read "Made Expressly For."

Sales of Plymouth's suburban trinket boomed in '59, with 89,114 Furys helping Plymouth rank third in the industry and celebrate the company's 11-millionth vehicle. With serious power and looks to stop a speeding train, the Fury wowed God-fearing America. But that rakish impudence couldn't last, and by '61 the Fury's fins were tragically trimmed. In the annals of kitsch, this one goes down as a real honey.

**HEAVY-METAL VILLAIN**
Stephen King's 1983 black comedy *Christine* used a '58 Fury as a demonic monster that suffocates its victims and eludes destruction by magically reconstituting itself. On screen, the Fury certainly looks like one of the baddest cars on the block.

**ENGINE**
The 318cid V8 pushed out just 230 horses, but Chrysler was starting to beat the performance drum as hard as it could. Top speed hit three figures, and acceleration was also brisk. The sheer bulk of the car plus those skinny tires must have made things a touch scary at the limit.

**INTERIOR**
Inside was comic-book spaceship, with push buttons galore. Swiveling front seats on Sport Furys were aimed at portlier buyers. The unlovely padded steering wheel was a $12 option.

**REAR SPORT DECK**
*The optional trunk-lid appliqué spare tire cover was meant to make the car upscale, but it looked more like a trash-can lid.*

**STAR STATUS**
*The '59 Fury is rightly regarded as one of Virgil Exner's all-time masterpieces.*

### FINS
*Everyone had fins back in 1959, but the Fury's showed real class.*

### TASTEFUL FLAIR
Is that slogan tongue-in-cheek? Plymouth sold the Fury's bold lines as the perfect example of taste and discrimination. It could only happen in '59.

GOOD TASTE IS NEVER EXTREME

### HEADLIGHTS
*$40 optional electronic dipping for the headlights relieved the driver of yet one more little hardship.*

### LUXURY OPTIONS
*Optional extras ranged from power brakes and the Golden Commando V8 to two-tone paint and contoured floormats.*

### 1959 PLMOUTH FURY
Chrysler design chief Virgil Exner liked to see classic lines bolted onto modern cars, and the trunk-lid spare tire cover on the Fury is one example of this. The profile of this two-door hardtop shows off the Fury's fine proportions. The shape is dartlike, with a tense urgency of line. The sloping cockpit and tapering rear window melt deliciously into those frantic fins.

### FIERCE FRONT GRILLE
*Cross-slatted grille was all new for '59 and made the front end look like it could bite.*

## SPECIFICATIONS

**MODEL** 1959 Plymouth Fury
**PRODUCTION** 105,887 (all body styles and including Sport Furys)
**BODY STYLE** Two-door hardtop.
**CONSTRUCTION** Steel body and chassis.
**ENGINE** 318cid V8 (360cid V8 optional for Sport Fury).
**POWER OUTPUT** 230 bhp (Sport Fury 260 bhp, or 305 bhp with 360cid V8).
**TRANSMISSION** Three-speed manual with optional overdrive, optional three-speed TorqueFlite automatic, and PowerFlite automatic.
**SUSPENSION** *Front:* torsion bars; *Rear:* leaf springs.
**BRAKES** Front and rear drums, optional power assistance.
**MAXIMUM SPEED** 105–110 mph (169–177 km/h)
**0–60 MPH (0–96 KM/H)** 11 sec
**A.F.C.** 17 mpg (6 km/l)

HAWAII 1961
**89 · 851**
ALOHA STATE

# 1959 PONTIAC
## *Bonneville*

THE BONNY WAS
*MOTOR TREND*'S 1959
CAR OF THE YEAR

IN THE LATE '50S, Detroit was worried. Desperately trying to offer something fresh, manufacturers decided to hit the aspirational thirty-somethings with a new package of performance, substance, and style. Pontiac's "Wide Track" Bonneville of '59 was a sensation. General Manager Bunkie Knudsen gave the line an image of youth and power, and Wide Track became all the rage. *Car Life* picked the Bonneville as its "Best Buy" and so did consumers. By 1960, soaring sales had made Pontiac the third most successful company in the industry.

The prestige Bonneville was also a dream to drive. The 389cid V8 pushed out up to 345 horses and, when the Tri-Power mill was fitted, top speeds hit 125 mph (201 km/h). At 6 ft 4 in (1.93 m) wide, the Custom two-door hardtop wouldn't fit in the car wash. But nobody cared. In 1959, America spent $300 million on chewing gum, the supermarket was its temple, and the ad jingle its national anthem. A self-obsessed utopia of comfort and convenience was about to go horribly wrong.

**WILD AND WACKY**
Garish three-color striped upholstery was meant to give the Bonneville a jaunty carelessness and appeal to the young at heart. Warehouse-like interior dimensions made it a true six-seater.

**DOUBLE FINS**
*With consumers crying out for individuality, Pontiac gave the Bonneville not two fins, but four.*

**GRILLE**
*The split grille was new for '59. After reverting back to a full-length grille for just one year, it became a Pontiac trademark in the early '60s.*

**INTERIOR**
The riotous interior had as much chrome as the exterior, and buyers could specify Wonderbar radio, electric antenna, tinted glass, padded dash, and tissue dispenser. The under-dash air-conditioning unit is a later, optional accessory.

### DASHBOARD
The "Astra-Dome" instrumentation was illuminated at night by electro-luminescent light, giving a soft, eerie glow that shone through the translucent markings on the gauges. It was technically very daring and boasted six different laminations of plastic, creating a rich, lustrous finish.

### THE ONLY BLEMISH
The much-criticized fake spare-tire embellishment on the trunk was variously described as a toilet seat or trash-can lid. Possibly the 300F's only stylistic peccadillo, it was dropped in '61.

TACHOMETER CAME AS STANDARD

### HUMONGOUS TRUNK
The two-door shape meant that the rear deck was the size of Indiana, and the cavernous trunk was large enough to hold four wheels and tires.

### SPECIFICATIONS

**MODEL** 1960 Chrysler 300F
**PRODUCTION** 1,212 (both body styles)
**BODY STYLE** Two-door coupe and convertible.
**CONSTRUCTION** Steel unitary body.
**ENGINE** 413cid V8.
**POWER OUTPUT** 375–400 bhp.
**TRANSMISSION** Three-speed push-button automatic, optional four-speed manual.
**SUSPENSION** *Front:* torsion bars; *Rear:* leaf springs.
**BRAKES** Front and rear drums.
**MAXIMUM SPEED** 140 mph (225 km/h)
**0–60 MPH** (0–96 KM/H) 7.1 sec
**A.F.C.** 12 mpg (4.2 km/l)

THIS PARTICULAR MODEL HAS SURE-GRIP DIFFERENTIAL, A $52 OPTION

### LENGTHY FINS
You could argue that the 300F's fins started at the front of the car and traveled along the side, building up to lethal, daggerlike points above the exquisitely sculptured taillights. Within two years fins would disappear completely on the Chrysler letter series 300.

POWER ANTENNA WAS A $43 OPTION, AND THIS CAR ALSO HAS THE GOLDEN TONE RADIO ($124) WITH REAR SEAT SPEAKER ($17)

NYLON WHITEWALLS CAME AS STANDARD

## EVOLUTION OF THE CHRYSLER 300 LETTER SERIES

THE 300 SERIES started life in 1955 when Chrysler came up with the first production sedan to kick out 300 bhp. The following year it was given the designation "B," and horsepower was hiked to 340. In '57 it became the 300C, pushing out 375 horses, and by '59 the "D" was producing 380 bhp. The only 300 without a letter was the '63, which would have read as a rather confusing 300I. Otherwise, the series followed in alphabetical order, the distinguished line culminating in the 360 bhp 300L of 1965.

RED HOT AND RAMBUNCTIOUS! 300/F BY CHRYSLER

ADVERTISING FOR THE 300F CALLED IT "THE SIXTH OF A FAMOUS FAMILY" AND "LEADER OF THE CLAN"

### 1955

AMERICA'S ORIGINAL muscle machine debuted as the C300, an image car to lock horns with the Corvette and T-Bird. Chrysler couldn't afford a two-seater, so instead stuffed everything it could into a New Yorker body. With a special Hemi and twin WCFB carbs, it was the fastest production car in the world and became known as "the car that swept Daytona."

**KEY FEATURES**
- Hand-built cars
- Oversize exhaust and solid valve lifters
- Only available in black, red, or white
- Base price of $4,055
- Options list runs to only 10 features

### 1956

THE 300B WAS THE first of the letter cars that gave buyers a choice of engine and transmission options. The base 354cid kicked out 340 horses, but mid-year a 355 bhp motor was offered, along with three different transmissions. The 300B, not Chevy's fuelie 283, was the first American engine to offer a genuine one horsepower per cubic inch.

**KEY DEVELOPMENTS**
- Revised rear end with new bumper and taillights
- Two-speed PowerFlite, TorqueFlite, and three-speed manual offered from mid-year
- Base price of $4,312
- Air-conditioning, record player, and clock set in steering wheel become options

## 1960 CHRYSLER *300F*

**BADGE**
The brazen red, white, and blue 300F badge on the rear wing left nobody in any doubt that this was really a thunderbolt in drag.

**SHARP END**
The 300F's razor-sharp rear fins were cited by Ralph Nader in his book *Unsafe at Any Speed* as "potentially lethal." In 1963, a motorcyclist hit the rear bumper of a 300F at speed and was impaled on the fin.

AIR-CONDITIONING COST A HEFTY $510 EXTRA

AUTOMATIC TRANSMISSION WAS ACTUATED BY PUSH-BUTTONS ON THE DASH

QUESTIONABLE REAR DECK TREATMENT WAS KNOWN AS "FLIGHT-SWEEP" AND WAS ALSO AVAILABLE ON OTHER CHRYSLERS

LSU CENTENNIAL
83 138
13 LOUISIANA 60

### HIDDEN FILLER
*The fuel filler-cap lurks behind this hinged section of the anodized beauty panel. The panel itself highlights the car's width.*

### LIGHTS
*Large, round, rear-light cluster aped the T-Bird and appeared on the Falcon as well as the Fairlane, also debuting in 1962.*

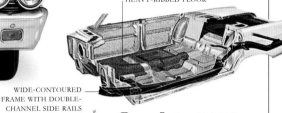

### ENGINE
Stock Galaxies lumbered around with a 223cid six or 292cid V8. The 500XL could choose from a range of Thunderbird V8s that included the 390cid Special, as here, and a 405 bhp 406cid V8 with triple Holley carbs, which could be ordered for $379.

---

## SPECIFICATIONS

**MODEL** 1962 Ford Galaxie 500XL Sunliner Convertible
**PRODUCTION** 13,183
**BODY STYLE** Two-door convertible.
**CONSTRUCTION** Steel body and chassis.
**ENGINE** 292cid, 352cid, 390cid, 406cid V8s.
**POWER OUTPUT** 170–405 bhp.
**TRANSMISSION** Three-speed Cruise-O-Matic automatic, optional four-speed manual.
**SUSPENSION** *Front:* coil springs; *Rear:* leaf springs.
**BRAKES** Front and rear drums.
**MAXIMUM SPEED** 108–140 mph (174–225 km/h)
**0–60 MPH (0–96 KM/H)** 7.6–14.2 sec
**A.F.C.** 16–18 mpg (5.7–6.4 km/l)

---

## 1962 FORD GALAXIE 500XL SUNLINER

The slab-sided Galaxie body was completely new for '62 and would set something of a styling trend for larger cars. Lines may have been flat and unadorned, but buyers could choose from 13 colors and 21 jaunty two-tones. The hardtop version of the 500XL Sunliner was the Club Victoria, $250 cheaper than the convertible and twice as popular, with 28,000 manufactured in '62.

HEAVY-RIBBED FLOOR

WIDE-CONTOURED FRAME WITH DOUBLE-CHANNEL SIDE RAILS

### BODY INSULATION
The Galaxie had an especially quiet ride because it was soundproofed at various points. Sound-absorbent mastic was applied to the inside surfaces of the doors, hood, trunk lid, fenders, and quarter panels, and thick fiberglass "blankets" insulated the roof.

### TOP UP
*Unlike this example, the rarest Sunliners have a wind-cheating Starlift hardtop, which was not on the options list.*

# 1962 FORD
## *Thunderbird*

IT WAS NO ACCIDENT THAT THE third-generation T-Bird looked like it was fired from a rocket silo. Designer Bill Boyer wanted the new prodigy to have "an aircraft and missilelike shape," a subtext that wasn't lost on an American public vexed by the Cuban crisis and Khrushchev's declaration of an increase in Soviet military spending.

THUNDERBIRDS ARE GO

The Sports Roadster model was the finest incarnation of the 1961–63 Thunderbird. With Kelsey-Hayes wire wheels and a two-seater fiberglass tonneau, it was one of the most glamorous cars on the block and one of the most exclusive. Virile, vast, and expensive, the Big Bird showed that Detroit still wasn't disposed to make smaller, cheaper cars. GM even impudently asserted that "a good used car is the only answer to America's need for cheap transportation." And building cars that looked and went like ballistic missiles was far more interesting and profitable.

**INTERIOR**
Aircraft imagery in the controls is obvious. The interior was designed around a prominent center console that split the cabin into two separate cockpits, delineating positions of driver and passenger. T-Bird drivers weren't that young, and a Swing-Away steering wheel *(left)* aided access for the more corpulent driver.

STANDARD POWER STEERING NEEDED JUST THREE-AND-A-HALF TURNS LOCK-TO-LOCK

CONSTRUCTION WAS DUAL-UNITIZED, WITH SEPARATE FRONT AND REAR SECTIONS WELDED TOGETHER AT THE COWL

**ROOF FUN**
With the top down, the streamlined tonneau made the Sports Roadster sleek enough to echo the '55 two-seater Thunderbird.

TINTED GLASS, POWER SEATS AND WINDOWS, AND AM/FM RADIO WERE THE MOST POPULAR OPTIONS

## 1963 STUDEBAKER AVANTI

More European than American, the Avanti had a long neck, razor-edged front fenders, and no grille. Early sketches show Loewy's inspiration, with telltale annotations scribbled on the paper that read "like Jaguar, Ferrari, Aston Martin, Mercedes." Lead time for the show Avanti was a hair-raising 13 months, with a full-scale clay model fashioned in only 40 days. Production estimates were as optimistic as 1,000 a month, but in the whole of 1964 Studebaker managed to churn out only 800 Avantis.

### REAR VIEW
Hardly dated at all, the rear view is clean, uncluttered, and very modern. Note the ageless rear light treatment.

### FRONT VIEW
Unmistakable from any angle, early '63 Avantis had round headlights, but most later '64 models sported square ones.

### SPECIFICATIONS

MODEL 1963 Studebaker Avanti
PRODUCTION 3,834
BODY STYLE Two-door, four-seater coupe.
CONSTRUCTION Fiberglass body, steel chassis.
ENGINE 289cid, 304cid V8s.
POWER OUTPUT 240–575 bhp (304cid R5 V8 fuel-injected).
TRANSMISSION Three-speed manual, optional Power-Shift automatic.
SUSPENSION *Front:* upper and lower A-arms, coil springs; *Rear:* leaf springs.
BRAKES Front discs, rear drums.
MAXIMUM SPEED 120 mph (193 km/h)
0–60 MPH (0–96 KM/H) 7.5 sec
A.F.C. 17 mpg (6 km/l)

# 1964 BUICK
## *Riviera*

BUICK'S '63 RIV WAS HAILED
AS A CONTEMPORARY CLASSIC

IN '58, SO THE STORY GOES, GM's design supremo Bill Mitchell was entranced by a Rolls-Royce he saw hissing past a London hotel. "What we want," said Mitchell, "is a cross between a Ferrari and a Rolls." By August 1960, he'd turned his vision into a full-size clay mock-up.

One of the world's most handsome cars, the original '63 Riviera was GM's attempt at a "Great New American Classic Car." And it worked. The elegant Riv was a clever amalgam of razor edges and chaste curves, embellished by just the right amount of chrome. Beneath the exquisite lines was a cross-member frame, a 401cid V8, power brakes, and a two-speed Turbine Drive tranny. In the interests of exclusivity, Buick agreed that only 40,000 would be made each year. With ravishing looks, prodigious performance, and the classiest image in town, the Riv ranks as one of Detroit's finest confections.

**INTERIOR**
The sumptuous Riv was a full four-seater, with the rear seat divided to look like buckets. The dominant V-shaped center console mushroomed from between the front seats to blend into the dashboard. The car's interior has a European ambience uncharacteristic for the period.

**DIMENSIONS**
*Relatively compact, the Riviera was considerably shorter and lighter than other big Buicks.*

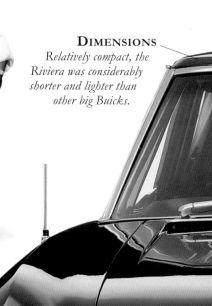

**CONWAY TWITTY**
The crooner of tunes like "It's Only Make Believe" owned the '64 Riv featured on these pages. Aimed at GM's most affluent customers, the Riviera soon became the American Jaguar.

**ENGINE**
'64s had a 425cid Wildcat V8 that could be tickled up to 360 horses courtesy of dual four-barrels. *Car Life* magazine tested a '64 Riv with the Wildcat and stomped to 60 mph (96 km/h) in a scintillating 7.7 seconds. Buick sold the tooling for the old 401 to Rover, which used it to great success in its Range Rover.

**SMART FRONT**
*The purposeful W-section front could have come straight out of an Italian styling house.*

**TRUNK SPACE**
*The substantial trunk could take two sets of golf clubs with ease, testimony to the leisure lifestyle of the average Riviera owner.*

## 1964 BUICK RIVIERA

The Riv was America's answer to the Bentley Continental, and pandered to Ivy League America's obsession with aristocratic European thoroughbreds like Aston Martin, Maserati, and Jaguar. The grille was inspired by the Ferrari 250GT, and the hard-edged fender line predated the angular Rolls-Royce Silver Shadow by three years. The rear view was a study in simplicity, with an unembellished trunk and delicate rear lights.

**DECORATION**
*Ineffectual side scoops weren't there to cool the rear brakes; they are the Riviera's only concession to vanity and disappeared in '65.*

**TRUNK LID**
*One optional extra was a remote-controlled trunk lid, which was pretty neat for '64.*

### SPECIFICATIONS

**MODEL** 1964 Buick Riviera
**PRODUCTION** 37,958
**BODY STYLE** Two-door hardtop coupe.
**CONSTRUCTION** Steel body and chassis.
**ENGINE** 425cid V8.
**POWER OUTPUT** 340–360 bhp.
**TRANSMISSION** Two- or three-speed automatic.
**SUSPENSION** Front and rear coil springs.
**BRAKES** Front and rear drums.
**MAXIMUM SPEED** 120–125 mph (193–201 km/h)
**0–60 MPH (0–96 KM/H)** 8 sec
**A.F.C.** 12–16 mpg (4.2–5.7 km/l)

**HEADLIGHTS**
*'63 and '64 Rivs have classic exposed double headlights. For reasons best known to themselves, Buick gave '65 cars headlights that were hidden behind electrically operated, clamshell doors.*

# 1964 LINCOLN
## *Continental*

CONTINENTAL ORNAMENT
WAS A MARK OF ESTEEM

THERE'S AN UNSETTLING irony in the fact that John F. Kennedy was shot in a '61 Lincoln Continental. Like him, the revamped '61 Continental had a new integrity. Substantial and innovative, it was bristling with new ideas and survived for nine years without major change.

The car fit for presidents was elegant, restrained, and classically sculptured, perfect for Camelot's new dynasty of liberalism. Ironic, too, that JFK rather liked the Lincoln – he often used a stock White House Continental for non-official business.

Nearly $7,000 bought one of the most influential and best-built American cars of the Sixties. It carried a two-year, 24,000-mile warranty, every engine was bench-tested, and each car given a 200-category shakedown. Ivy League America approved, and production doubled in the first year. Even the Industrial Design Institute was impressed, awarding its coveted bronze medal for "an outstanding contribution of simplicity and design elegance."

## PRESIDENTIAL WHEELS

THE DARK BLUE 1961 Continental phaeton, watched by the world in Dallas was on loan to the White House from Ford's Special Vehicles Division for $500 a year. It had rear seats that could be raised or lowered automatically, two-way radio telephone, and thick steel-plating along the front and rear side rails. After the November 1963 assassination, it was still kept in harness, serving both the Johnson and Nixon administrations. Later fitted with a permanent solid roof, it was eventually retired to the Henry Ford Museum in Dearborn, where it still resides.

JFK IN THE PRESIDENTIAL CONTINENTAL ON THE DAY OF
HIS ASSASSINATION IN DALLAS

GAUGES SHOWING FUEL SUPPLY, OIL
PRESSURE, WATER TEMPERATURE, AND
BATTERY CHARGE WERE NEW FOR '64

### INTERIOR
Every Continental had power steering and windows, walnut cappings, a padded dashboard, lush carpets, and vacuum-powered door locks as standard. The locks operated automatically as soon as the car started to move.

SUSPENSION
DAMPING WAS
CONSIDERED
THE BEST ON
ANY CAR

### ENGINE
Power was supplied by a huge 430cid V8 that generated 320 bhp. Each engine was tested at near maximum revs for three hours and then stripped down for inspection. Many mechanical parts were sealed for life.

MASSIVE
WINDSHIELD
GAVE
EXCELLENT
ALL-AROUND
VISION

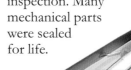

TO SPREAD COSTS, THE CONTINENTAL SHARED SOME OF ITS FACTORY TOOLING WITH THE '61 THUNDERBIRD

## LINEAR PROFILE
Apart from the gentle dip in the waistline at the back of the rear doors, the roof and fender lines form two uninterrupted, almost parallel lines.

## STATE-OF-THE-ART TOP
Eleven relays and a maze of linkages made the Continental's top disappear neatly into the trunk. The electric systems were completely sealed and never needed maintenance.

## CONVERTIBLE RARITIES
Ragtop Continentals were really "convertible sedans" with standard power tops. The '64 ragtops were stickered at only $646 more than the four-door sedans, yet they remain much rarer models: only about 10 percent of all '61–'67 Lincolns produced were convertibles.

## SPECIFICATIONS

**MODEL** 1964 Lincoln Continental Convertible
**PRODUCTION** 3,328
**BODY STYLE** Four-door, five-seater convertible.
**CONSTRUCTION** Steel body and chassis.
**ENGINE** 430cid V8.
**POWER OUTPUT** 320 bhp.
**TRANSMISSION** Three-speed Turbo-Drive automatic.
**SUSPENSION** *Front:* control arms and coil springs; *Rear:* leaf springs with live axle.
**BRAKES** Front and rear drums.
**MAXIMUM SPEED** 115 mph (185 km/h)
**0–60 MPH (0–96 KM/H)** 11 sec
**A.F.C.** 14 mpg (5 km/l)

## EASY ACCESS
The "suicide" rear-hinged doors hark back to classic prewar coachbuilding. On older Continental Convertibles, opening all four doors at once can actually bend the floor and chassis.

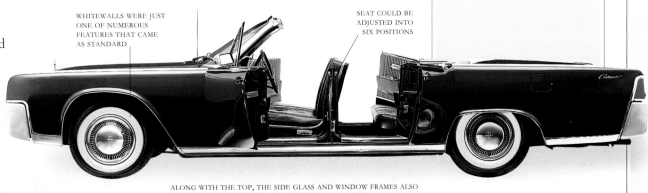

WHITEWALLS WERE JUST ONE OF NUMEROUS FEATURES THAT CAME AS STANDARD

SEAT COULD BE ADJUSTED INTO SIX POSITIONS

ALONG WITH THE TOP, THE SIDE GLASS AND WINDOW FRAMES ALSO DISAPPEARED FROM VIEW AT THE TOUCH OF A BUTTON

# EVOLUTION OF THE LINCOLN CONTINENTAL

THE REVOLUTIONARY Continental of 1961 ranks as one of Detroit's greatest achievements. Chiseled good looks, enviably precise tolerances, and an exclusive bloodline made it the most desirable Lincoln since the prewar K-Series. Sixties Continentals were the pre-eminent American luxury car and had an aura of distinction that stood out from the garish autos of the Fifties. Today it stands as evidence that, when they tried, Detroit could match the best in the world.

## 1940

1940 WAS THE FIRST YEAR of the Continental, a European shape based on the Lincoln Zephyr. With both coupe and convertible retailing at just under $3,000, the nation sighed in admiration at Ford's new dreamboat. By 1941 the Continental became a model in its own right. One of America's most prestigious brands had been born.

### KEY FEATURES
- First cars powered by Lincoln's unreliable L-head V12
- Push-button exterior door handles in '41
- New 305cid V12 in '42, along with face-lift that gives Continental longer, higher wings, and new nose
- Headlights now flanked by parking lights

## 1956

OFFERED ONLY AS a two-door model with a stratospheric price tag of $10,000, nobody expected the Mark II of 1956 to sell seriously. The comely Continental was a flagship car intended to bless other Ford products with a halo of association. And it worked. In its day the Mark II was distinguished, beautiful, and made by Uncle Henry.

### KEY DEVELOPMENTS
- Launched at the 1955 Paris Auto Show to universal acclaim
- Special Continental Division created to market the Mark II
- All options standard except air-conditioning
- Only 2,994 sold

## 1961

LINCOLN BUILT YET another landmark car with the '61 Mark III. Bold, stylish, and influential, it scooped every award going. Bristling with quality and oozing class, the Camelot Continental set new standards of US automobile engineering integrity. Lincoln wisely kept the classic shape current, with only gentle styling changes up until 1969.

### KEY DEVELOPMENTS
- Automatic transmission, radio, power brakes, steering, and windows all standard
- Mild styling tweaks until major face-lift in '65, but retains basic '61 shape
- '66 sees taillights no longer wrapping around bumper
- Gentle redesign in '68, with new hood

# 1964 LINCOLN
## *Continental*

IN '61, LINCOLN WAS THE ONLY MANUFACTURER TO OFFER A FOUR-DOOR CONVERTIBLE

LEAST POPULAR OPTION IN '64 WAS THE ADJUSTABLE STEERING WHEEL

## QUALITY NOT QUANTITY
The '61 restyle reflected the new philosophy that big was not necessarily better. The previous Conti was a leviathan, but not so the '61. Lincoln historian James Wagner described the '61 Continental as "more like a Mercedes-Benz than a product of General Motors."

## 1972

LONGER, LOWER, wider, and heavier than the Mark III Continental, the Mark IV, from '70 on, still had the same sharp shape. It was based on the T-Bird and that big 460cid lived up front, albeit detuned to a paltry 200 bhp because of emission controls. In spite of the energy crisis, it sold even better than the Mark III, averaging 50,000 to 60,000 each year.

**KEY DEVELOPMENTS**
- New crisscross pattern grille
- New roof design with oblong opera window
- Increased leg and shoulder room for rear-seat passengers
- Cartier electric clock as standard

## 1984

A MARK VII COUPE joined the mid-sized Continental for '84, both with all-disc brakes and two industry firsts: gas-pressurized shock absorbers and self-sealing tires. There was also a Mark VII LSC with a performance package. The Mark VII was a credible alternative to the Cadillac Seville and Eldorado, and the LSC in particular was a very quick car.

**KEY DEVELOPMENTS**
- Auto-leveling electronic air suspension standard in '84
- Two-door coupe joins lineup in '84
- LSC gains high output V8 for '85
- ABS standard in '86
- 302cid V8 gets sequential fuel injection in '86

## 1988

THE ALL-NEW CONTINENTAL for '88 was the first Lincoln with front-wheel drive and a six-cylinder mill. Weight was down but length was up. The only available engine was the 232cid V6 with four-speed overdrive automatic, not really powerful enough for such a big old tank. Computer-controlled suspension adjusted for changes in the road.

**KEY DEVELOPMENTS**
- Increased interior and trunk space
- Now a genuine six-seater
- Electronic dash attracts criticism and is revised in '89
- His and her airbags for '89
- Dual exhausts for '89

## 1995

AFTER A MODERATE restyle in '94, '95 saw a major overhaul. Aside from the exterior design changes and a new 260 bhp V8, a dazzling array of high-tech features included the ability to program ride, transmission, handling, and interior setup to suit each individual driver. This was truly a car to take Lincoln into the 21st century.

**KEY DEVELOPMENTS**
- New unibody design
- New 32-valve InTech™ V8 is first Ford block to be placed in transverse mounting position
- New nonsynchro four-speed automatic gearbox allows quicker shifting
- 100,000 mile (161,000 km) tune-up interval

**COMPETITION BEATER**
Low, wide, and mighty, the '60s Continental was considered the epitome of good taste and discrimination, and a patriotic alternative to the less sophisticated and poorly built Jaguar Mark 10 sedan.

TINTED GLASS WAS A $53 OPTIONAL EXTRA

EVEN IN '64 YOU COULD HAVE CRUISE CONTROL, FOR A MERE $96 EXTRA

HEADLIGHTS COULD SENSE ONCOMING TRAFFIC AND DIM AUTOMATICALLY

NEW YORK
KTS 340
LINCOLN
1964

# 1964 OLDSMOBILE
## *Starfire*

'64 OLDSMOBILES WERE MARKETED WITH
THE SLOGAN, "WHERE THE ACTION IS"

IN 1964, LBJ SIGNED A tax-cut bill, *Peyton Place* was a TV hit, and Coca-Cola launched a new single-calorie soda called Tab. While America was on a roll, the auto industry was busy telling customers that bucket seats and center consoles would enrich their lives. Oldsmobile trumpeted that its sporty Starfire Coupe offered "high adventure that starts right here!" Lame copy aside, the Starfire was quick, with Olds' most powerful lump, a 394cid V8 that could knock on the door of 120 mph (193 km/h). A terrifying thirst for gas didn't deter buyers, especially since these were big, softly sprung mile-eaters, groaning with convenience options. Elegant and unadorned, the Starfire was one of a new breed of suburban starlets designed to make the American middle classes look as confident as they felt. And it worked.

## CONVERTIBLE OPTION
The Starfire was easy on the hands, with power everything. Detroit knew that the "little woman" was becoming increasingly important in buying decisions and started to pitch their products at the shopping mall. Early Starfires were available only in convertible form and came with a special engine and deluxe interior.

## ENGINE
Standard on the Starfire Coupe and Convertible was the mighty cast-iron block 394cid V8 with Rochester four-barrel carb, which churned out a hefty 345 bhp. Performance on original '61 models was positively exhilarating, but three years down the line the effect of all those sybaritic creature comforts and added weight meant that the Starfire wasn't that quick, and speed figures ended up this side of ordinary.

## WEIGHT
*The Starfire was no featherweight; all those luxury add-ons pushed the curb weight to nearly two tons.*

TILT STEERING WAS
AN OPTION AT $43

## INTERIOR
Oldsmobile gave the Starfire plenty of creature comforts. Standard kit included Hydra-Matic automatic transmission, bucket seats, safety padded dash, center console, tachometer, leather trim, plus power steering, brakes, and windows. The power seat could be adjusted into six positions and the Tilt-Away steering wheel into seven.

## 1964 OLDSMOBILE STARFIRE

Based on the body shell of the Dynamic 88, the Starfire never looked special enough to win big sales. *Motor Trend* said: "What the Starfire misses most is a distinctive exterior like the Thunderbird." Nevertheless, they did describe the 120 mph (193 km/h) oily bits as "superior and sensational." The car's simple, extruded look was typical of the period, and very few traces of jukebox styling remained by the mid-Sixties. Lines were clean and assertive, appealing to the affluent society's newfound sophistication.

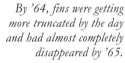

### ANTISPIN OPTION
*Positive-traction rear axle was a factory-fitted option.*

### FINS
*By '64, fins were getting more truncated by the day and had almost completely disappeared by '65.*

### HEADLIGHTS
*Guide-Matic headlights automatically dimmed for oncoming cars.*

### SPECIFICATIONS

**MODEL** 1964 Oldsmobile Starfire
**PRODUCTION** 25,890
**BODY STYLE** Two-door, five-seater coupe and convertible.
**CONSTRUCTION** Steel body and chassis.
**ENGINE** 394cid V8.
**POWER OUTPUT** 345 bhp.
**TRANSMISSION** Three-speed Hydra-Matic automatic.
**SUSPENSION** Front and rear coil springs.
**BRAKES** Front and rear drums.
**MAXIMUM SPEED** 120 mph (193 km/h)
**0–60 MPH (0–96 KM/H)** 9 sec
**A.F.C.** 12 mpg (4.2 km/l)

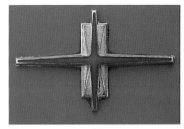

### OLDSMOBILE BADGE
The Starfire name originally belonged to a jet fighter, and GM sold it as a limited edition upscale personal car. Sales began to dwindle by 1965, when it was eclipsed by the Buick Riviera. By 1967, the Starfire had been replaced by the Oldsmobile Toronado.

### WHEELBASE
*The Starfire was based on the Dynamic 88 and shared its 123 in (312 cm) wheelbase.*

# 1964 PLYMOUTH
## *Barracuda*

**Did you know**

that the 1965 Plymouth Barracuda has an optional Formula 'S' sports package that includes a Commando 273-cu.-in. V-8 engine'; heavy-duty shocks, springs, and sway bar; a tachometer; wide-rim (14-in.) wheels, special Blue Streak tires, and simulated bolt-on wheel covers?

**You do now.**

THE ROARING '65s
FURY
BELVEDERE
VALIANT
BARRACUDA

*ROAD AND TRACK MAGAZINE SAID, "FOR SPORTS CAR PERFORMANCE AND PRACTICALITY, THE BARRACUDA IS PERFECT"*

THE BIG THREE WEREN'T slow to cash in on the Sixties' youth boom. Ford couldn't keep its Mustang project secret, and the Chrysler Corporation desperately wanted a piece of the action. To get the drop on Uncle Henry, the company had to work fast. It took its existing compact, the Plymouth Valiant, prettied up the front end, added a dramatic wraparound rear window, and called it the Barracuda. It hit the showroom carpets in April 1964, two weeks before the Mustang.

A disarming amalgam of performance, poise, and refinement, Plymouth had achieved a miracle on the scale of loaves and fishes: it made the Barracuda fast, yet handle crisply and ride smoothly. The 273cid V8 made the car quicker than a Mustang, faster still if the new owner had specified the Formula S package. But that bizarre rear window dated fiercely, and Mustangs outsold Barracudas 10-to-one. Plymouth believed the long-hood/short-trunk "pony" formula wouldn't captivate consumers like a swooping, sporty fastback. Half a million Mustang buyers told them they'd backed the wrong horse.

### THE FORMULA S OPTION

Despite the fact that the Formula S offered a V8 block plus race trimmings, this was still rather tame by Plymouth standards. The '61 Fury, for example, had a 318cid unit that pushed out 230 bhp.

### BARRACUDA EXTRAS

Options were not as extensive as on the Mustang, but you could still add air-conditioning, TorqueFlite automatic transmission, and sport wheel covers with chrome lugs to the Barracuda's $2,500 base price.

### ENGINE

The 'Cuda's base engine was a 170cid slant six. Other mills were the 225cid six and two-barrel 273cid V8. Optional was Chrysler's new Hurst-linkage manual transmission along with new Sure-Grip differential.

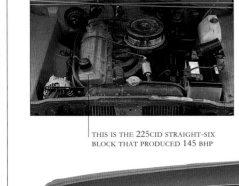

THIS IS THE 225CID STRAIGHT-SIX BLOCK THAT PRODUCED 145 BHP

OPTIONAL POWER STEERING MEANT THAT LOCK-TO-LOCK WAS ONLY THREE-AND-A-HALF TURNS

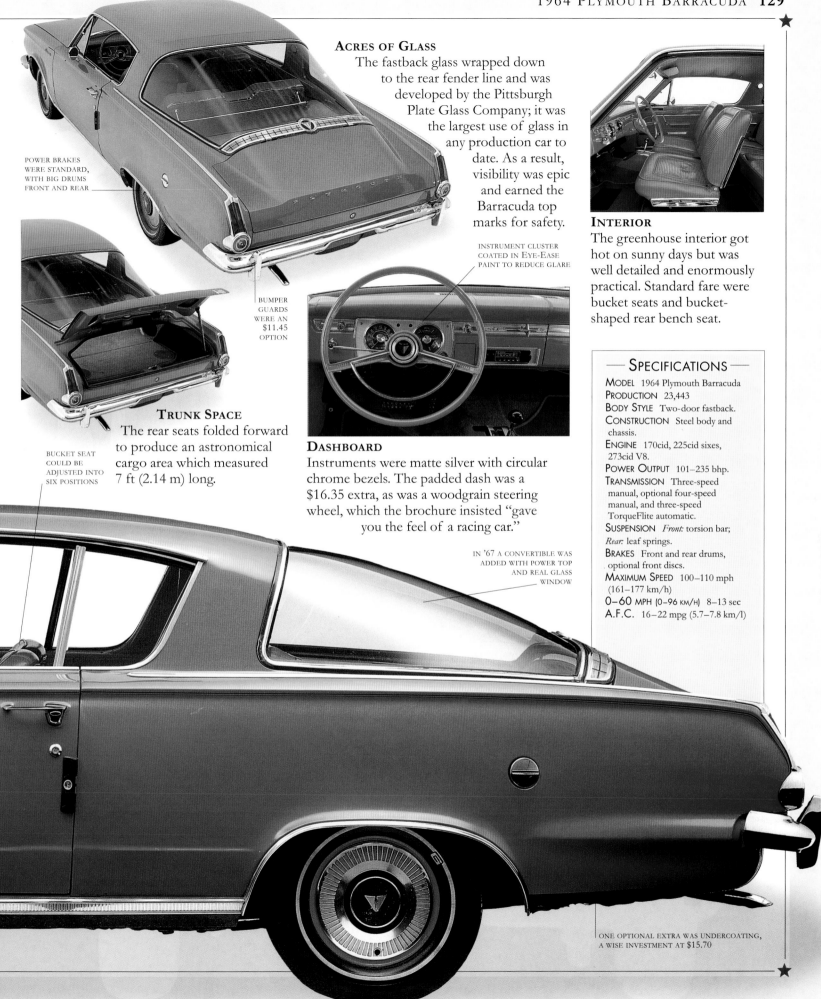

## ACRES OF GLASS

The fastback glass wrapped down to the rear fender line and was developed by the Pittsburgh Plate Glass Company; it was the largest use of glass in any production car to date. As a result, visibility was epic and earned the Barracuda top marks for safety.

POWER BRAKES WERE STANDARD, WITH BIG DRUMS FRONT AND REAR

BUMPER GUARDS WERE AN $11.45 OPTION

INSTRUMENT CLUSTER COATED IN EYE-EASE PAINT TO REDUCE GLARE

## INTERIOR

The greenhouse interior got hot on sunny days but was well detailed and enormously practical. Standard fare were bucket seats and bucket-shaped rear bench seat.

## TRUNK SPACE

The rear seats folded forward to produce an astronomical cargo area which measured 7 ft (2.14 m) long.

BUCKET SEAT COULD BE ADJUSTED INTO SIX POSITIONS

## DASHBOARD

Instruments were matte silver with circular chrome bezels. The padded dash was a $16.35 extra, as was a woodgrain steering wheel, which the brochure insisted "gave you the feel of a racing car."

IN '67 A CONVERTIBLE WAS ADDED WITH POWER TOP AND REAL GLASS WINDOW

### SPECIFICATIONS

**MODEL** 1964 Plymouth Barracuda
**PRODUCTION** 23,443
**BODY STYLE** Two-door fastback.
**CONSTRUCTION** Steel body and chassis.
**ENGINE** 170cid, 225cid sixes, 273cid V8.
**POWER OUTPUT** 101–235 bhp.
**TRANSMISSION** Three-speed manual, optional four-speed manual, and three-speed TorqueFlite automatic.
**SUSPENSION** *Front:* torsion bar; *Rear:* leaf springs.
**BRAKES** Front and rear drums, optional front discs.
**MAXIMUM SPEED** 100–110 mph (161–177 km/h)
**0–60 MPH (0–96 KM/H)** 8–13 sec
**A.F.C.** 16–22 mpg (5.7–7.8 km/l)

ONE OPTIONAL EXTRA WAS UNDERCOATING, A WISE INVESTMENT AT $15.70

# MUSCLE AND PONY MANIA

BY THE EARLY SIXTIES, buyers were bored with overchromed barges, gas was cheap, and the economy was thumping. Two types of badly needed automotive narcotic were about to emerge – the pony car and the muscle car. The first real muscle cars were the '62 Plymouths and Dodges, with their wedge-head V8s, but the machine that really defined the breed was John DeLorean's hip '64 Pontiac GTO. Stripped to the bone, it was a street-legal screamer with blistering straight-line heave, and sales went absolutely ballistic.

Ford got in on the act with its hot Fairlane and Shelby Mustang, Oldsmobile placed a

THE FIRST BARRACUDAS WERE ACTUALLY QUITE GENTEEL

performance package in the F-85 and called it the 4-4-2, and Chrysler followed by stuffing Hemi engines into everything it could. The muscle car was hot news on the street because it promised not only horsepower, but individuality, too. With a landslide of performance options, auto makers let buyers kid themselves that their cars were almost custom-made. One ad for the Dodge Challenger boasted, "This is a car you buy when you decide you don't want to be like everyone else."

Plymouth was too late with the '64 Barracuda to cash in on the muscle-car mania, but by '68 things were really cooking with special performance packages and a monster 440cid mill

EARLY MUSTANG PROTOTYPE WAS A PROMISE OF PERFORMANCE TO COME

PRESENTING THE *Mustang* by Ford Engineers and Stylists

## 1964 PLYMOUTH
### *Barracuda*

THE BARRACUDA WAS A PLYMOUTH VALIANT FROM THE ROOF LINE DOWN AND SHARED ITS POWER AND SUSPENSION

**VEHICLE NUMBER**
This was located on a plate on the front left doorpost and became visible when the door was opened.

**YOUTH MARKET**
Based on the mass-market, best-selling Valiant, the Barracuda was aimed at a completely new market: rich young things with a desire to look cool.

19 400TH ANNIVERSARY 65
1W 166142
FLORIDA

**TURN SIGNALS**
*Turn signals in the grille were meant to mimic European-style driving lights.*

**HEADLIGHTS**
*The stacked headlights were new for Pontiacs in '65 and were retained on GTOs until the end of the decade.*

### SPECIFICATIONS

**MODEL** 1966 Pontiac GTO Convertible

**PRODUCTION** 96,946 (all body styles)

**BODY STYLE** Two-door, five-seater hardtop, coupe, and convertible.

**CONSTRUCTION** Steel unitary body.

**ENGINE** 389cid V8s.

**POWER OUTPUT** 335–360 bhp.

**TRANSMISSION** Three-speed manual, optional four-speed manual, and three-speed Hydra-Matic automatic.

**SUSPENSION** Front and rear coil springs.

**BRAKES** Front and rear drums, optional discs.

**MAXIMUM SPEED** 125 mph (201 km/h)

**0–60 MPH (0–96 KM/H)** 6.6–9.5 sec

**A.F.C.** 15 mpg (5.3 km/l)

## 1966 PONTIAC GTO CONVERTIBLE

John DeLorean's idea of placing a high-spec engine in the standard Tempest body paved the way for a whole new genre and gave Pontiac immediate success in '64. Had Ford not chosen to release the Mustang in the same year, the GTO would have been the star of '64, and even more sales would have been secured. As it was, sales peaked in '66 with almost 100,000 GTOs going to power-hungry young drivers whose average age was 25. The Convertible was the most aesthetically pleasing of the range.

**PERFORMANCE REAR**
*The GTO came with heavy-duty shocks and springs as standard, along with a stabilizer bar.*

**LENGTH**
*It might look long, but the GTO was actually 15 in (38 cm) shorter than Pontiac's largest models.*

# 1967 FORD
## *Shelby Mustang GT500*

GT500 NAME WAS
ARBITRARY AND DID
NOT REFER TO POWER

LOOKING BACK FROM OUR ERA of weedy political correctness, it's amazing to remember a time when you could buy this sort of stomach-churning horsepower straight from the showroom floor. What's more, if you couldn't afford to buy it, you could borrow it for the weekend from your local Hertz rent-a-car. The fact is that the American public loved the grunt, the image, and the Carroll Shelby Cobra connection. Ford's advertising slogan went straight to the point – Shelby Mustangs were "*The* Road Cars." With 289 and 428cid V8s, they were blisteringly quick, kings of both street and strip. By '67 they were civilized, too, with options like factory air and power steering, as well as lots of gauges, a wood-rim Shelby wheel, and that all-important 140 mph (225 km/h) speedo. The little Pony Mustang had grown into a thundering stallion.

### DASHBOARD
The special Shelby steering wheel was standard, along with Stewart-Warner oil and amp gauges and a tachometer red-lining at 8,000 rpm. Two interior colors were available – parchment and black.

### CHUNKY FRONT
'67 Shelbys had a larger hood scoop than previous models, plus a custom-built fiberglass front to complement the stock Mustang's new longer hood.

WOOD-RIM STEERING WHEEL

### CARROLL SHELBY

CARROLL SHELBY, the most charismatic ex-chicken farmer you could ever meet, smiled when he told me the Hertz story. "We delivered the first batch of black-and-gold cars to Hertz the day before a hailstorm. The cars had racing brakes that really needed carefully warming up. When the ice storm hit, dozens were totaled. My reputation with Hertz went down the tubes big time." But the Hertz connection was good for the Shelby, and there are tales of people renting 350s and 500s for the weekend and bringing them back with bald tires and evidence of racing numbers on the doors. There was even one case of somebody lifting a 289 Hi-Po out of a Hertz Shelby and substituting the stock 289 from his aunt's notchback, hoping no one would notice.

CARROLL SHELBY RECEIVES HIS TROPHY FOR
WINNING THE RIVERSIDE GRAND PRIX IN 1960

INTERIOR DECOR WAS
BRUSHED ALUMINUM
WITH MOLDED DOOR
PANELS AND
DOOR
LIGHTS

SHELBY'S SPRINGING
WAS SIMILAR TO THE
MUSTANG WITH FRONT
SWAY BAR, STIFF SPRINGS,
AND GABRIEL SHOCKS

G.T. 500

## ENGINE

The GT500 had the 428 Police Interceptor unit with two Holley four-barrel carbs. Oval, finned aluminum open-element air cleaner and cast-aluminum valve covers were unique to the big-block Shelby.

## SHELBY PLATE

Carroll Shelby gave the early Mustangs his special treatment in a dedicated factory in Los Angeles. Later cars were built in Ionia, Michigan.

## INTERIOR

All GT350s and 500s boasted the standard and very practical Mustang fold-down rear seat along with Shelby's own padded roll bar. Shelbys came in fastback only; there were no notchbacks and convertibles were only available from '68 on.

## SPECIFICATIONS

**MODEL** 1967 Ford Shelby Cobra Mustang GT500
**PRODUCTION** 2,048
**BODY STYLE** Two-door, four-seater coupe.
**CONSTRUCTION** Steel unitary body.
**ENGINE** 428cid V8.
**POWER OUTPUT** 360 bhp.
**TRANSMISSION** Four-speed manual, three-speed automatic.
**SUSPENSION** *Front:* coil springs; *Rear:* leaf springs.
**BRAKES** Front discs, rear drums.
**MAXIMUM SPEED** 132 mph (212 km/h)
**0–60 MPH** (0–96 KM/H) 6.8 sec
**A.F.C.** 13 mpg (4.6 km/l)

SCOOPS ACTED AS INTERIOR AIR EXTRACTORS

REAR DECK IS MADE OF FIBERGLASS TO SAVE WEIGHT

## POPULAR CHOICE

Shelbys were a big hit in '67, with 1,175 350s and 2,048 500s sold. Prices were also about 15 percent cheaper than in '66.

WHEELS ARE OPTIONAL KELSEY-HAYES MAGSTARS

## EVOLUTION OF THE FORD MUSTANG

NO OTHER CAR HIT its target like the Mustang. Aimed at the 18–24 market, it was charismatic, youthful, and cheap; mass-produced individuality had never looked so good. With their litany of options, Mustangs could be everything from a secretary's economy compact to a street racer's howling banshee. Iacocca's prodigy may have spawned the Firebird and the Camaro, but its legacy is far greater than that. Thirty-odd years later, America still loves the galloping pony.

### 1962

THE MUSTANG'S ANTECEDENTS go back to the Project T5 styling study created in 1962 by engineer Herb Misch and design chief Eugene Bordinat. Meant to take on British Triumphs and MGs, it had independent springing, a tubular frame, integral roll bar, and a 60-degree 1927 cc V4 engine.

#### KEY FEATURES
- Ford backs sporty, compact Project T5
- Mustang styling exercises approved in just 21 days
- Target market is baby boomers
- Prototype debuts in time for US Grand Prix at Watkins Glen

### 1964

LAUNCHED IN APRIL 1964, the Mustang was such a colossal hit that production at the Dearborn factory couldn't cope and spilled over to the Ford plant in San Jose, California. By the end of the year the Pony had notched up 263,000 sales and the full calendar year production total for '65 of 418,000 units was an industry record.

#### KEY DEVELOPMENTS
- Early cars have 260cid V8s
- First batch has nonadjustable passenger seats
- Base price is an amazing $2,368
- Lee Iacocca makes the front cover of *Time* magazine

### 1969

THE MUSTANG QUICKLY put on weight and, far from being a compact, had grown into a luxury Grand Tourer. Mind you, power was up, too, with screamers like the Mach One and whopping Boss 429. Moving away from the pony-car philosophy wasn't one of Ford's best ideas, and '69 model year output fell to 190,727 units, down from 300,000.

#### KEY DEVELOPMENTS
- New sports roof fastback body style
- New ultra-high performance models Boss 302 and Boss 429
- Luxury Grandee model launched
- 81.5 percent of all '69 'Stangs have a V8

## 1967 FORD *Shelby Mustang GT500*

FOR THE SHELBY, THE MUSTANG'S REAR LIGHTS WERE REPLACED WITH THE '65 T-BIRD'S SEQUENTIAL LIGHTS

### MORE POWER AND CONTROL
Power steering and brakes on the '67 model meant that the once rough-riding Shelby had changed into a luxury slingshot.

19 GEORGIA STATE 67
USA 716
SHELBY

## 1971

THE MUSTANGS OF '71 grew in every dimension except for height. Heavier, wider, and more bloated than its lithe predecessors, the Mustang lost its way, and sales plummeted to nearly a third of '65–'66 numbers. Everybody knew that this wasn't the way to go, but over the following three years things would get even worse.

### KEY DEVELOPMENTS
• Boss 302 and 489 dropped in favor of Boss 351
• Standard base engine now a 250cid six

## 1974

APOLOGETICALLY BILLED AS "the right car at the right time," the Mustang II wasn't worthy of bearing the hallowed name. With parts borrowed from the subcompact Pinto, it was a knee-jerk reaction to the Arab oil embargo. Still, for all its ordinariness, sales were strong, with 385,000 Mustang IIs finding buyers in the first year.

### KEY DEVELOPMENTS
• New body designed by Ghia
• Now billed as a "luxury subcompact"
• Pared down four-model line-up
• Base engine is asthmatic 140cid four
• Mach One gets 171cid V6

## 1979

THE FIFTH-GENERATION Mustangs were clean, taut, and crisply styled. On the down side, handling wasn't great, interior space was limited, and build quality couldn't match the Japanese. The Iran–Iraq war meant that performance was out and economy was in, but the desire for power would soon return, and the Mustang would rise again.

### KEY DEVELOPMENTS
• New color-keyed urethane bumpers
• Heavy aerodynamic influence
• Wicked 302cid V8 option
• Cobra option has 2.3 turbo four

## 1993

1993 MUSTANGS WERE among the most civilized and refined of the breed. The 5-liter V8 was considered quick enough to make a highway patrol car, and the limited edition Mustang Cobra included GT40 heads and roller rockers. This incarnation kept the customers satisfied until the splendid all-new Mustang arrived on the scene in 1995.

### KEY DEVELOPMENTS
• Three body styles available in LX 5.0 guise
• Base models run on 88 bhp four
• Driver's airbag standard
• GT Mustangs push out 225 bhp

**FORCED CHANGES**
The standard center-grille high-beam headlights were forced to the sides in some states because of Federal legislation.

AT THE END OF '67, CARS WERE RENAMED SHELBY COBRAS, BUT FORD STILL HANDLED ALL PROMOTION AND ADVERTISING

SHELBY BODIES WERE NEW FOR '67, WITH A SHARKLIKE FRONT GRILLE AND UPDATED HOOD WITH RAM-AIR OPENINGS

428CID V8 STARTED LIFE IN THE ORIGINAL AC COBRA

RACING-STYLE LOCK PINS WERE STANDARD ON THE HOOD

SHELBY G.T. 500

APRIL GEORGIA STATE 1967
USA 716
SHELBY

# 1967 OLDSMOBILE
## *Toronado*

NARROW GRILLE WAS A TORO STYLING TRADEMARK

THE FIRST BIG FRONT-DRIVING LAND YACHT since the Cord 810 of the Thirties, the Toronado was an automotive milestone and the most desirable Olds ever. With a 425cid V8 and unique chain-and-sprocket-drive automatic transmission, it had big-car power and outstanding road manners, and it could crack 135 mph (217 km/h). Initial sales weren't great, with sober buyers plumping for the more conventional Riviera, but by '71 the Riviera's design had lost its way. Then the Toronado really came into its own, selling up to 50,000 a year until the mid-Seventies. From then on, however, the more glamorous Cadillac Eldorado, also with front drive, outsold both the Riviera and the Toronado. Built on an exclusive slow-moving assembly line, Toronados had few faults, which was remarkable for such a technically audacious car. Even so, the press carped about the poor rear visibility, lousy gas mileage, and voracious appetite for front tires. But time heals all wounds, and these days there's no greater collector's car bargain than a '66–'67 Toronado.

**NOVEL FRONTAL STYLE**
The concealed headlights and horizontal bar grille were genuinely innovative but would disappear in '68 for a heavier and less attractive front-end treatment. The Toronado's design arose in a free-expression competition organized by Olds in 1962. It became the marque's top model to date, and the equivalent of the Buick Riviera.

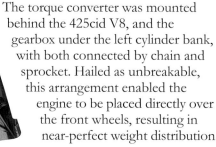

**TOP-FLIGHT CREDENTIALS**
The Toronado was brisk, poised, and accurate. Understeer and front-wheel scrabble were kept to a minimum, and the car handled like a compact. Acceleration was in the Jaguar sedan league, and flat out it could chew the tail feathers of a Hi-Po Mustang.

**ENGINE**
The torque converter was mounted behind the 425cid V8, and the gearbox under the left cylinder bank, with both connected by chain and sprocket. Hailed as unbreakable, this arrangement enabled the engine to be placed directly over the front wheels, resulting in near-perfect weight distribution.

FROM 1972 ON, TORONADOS WERE BUILT EXCLUSIVELY IN LANSING

THE TORONADO NAME CAME FROM A 1963 CHEVROLET SHOW CAR AND HAS NO KNOWN MEANING

### RACING IMAGE

The sporty checkered flag motif didn't really reflect the Monte's market place. Owners were respectable, middle-aged types with five-bedroom houses in upscale neighborhoods.

### SPECIFICATIONS

**MODEL** 1970 Chevrolet Monte Carlo
**PRODUCTION** 145,975
**BODY STYLE** Two-door, five-seater coupe.
**CONSTRUCTION** Steel body and chassis.
**ENGINE** 350cid, 400cid, 454cid V8s.
**POWER OUTPUT** 250–360 bhp.
**TRANSMISSION** Three-speed manual, optional two-speed Powerglide automatic, Turbo Hydra-Matic three-speed automatic.
**SUSPENSION** *Front:* coil springs; *Rear:* leaf springs.
**BRAKES** Front and rear drums.
**MAXIMUM SPEED** 115–132 mph (185–211 km/h)
**0–60 MPH** (0–96 KM/H) 8–14 sec
**A.F.C.** 15–20 mpg (5.3–7 km/l)

### 1970 CHEVROLET MONTE CARLO

The Monte Carlo used the same platform as the redesigned 1969 Pontiac Grand Prix. Stylistically, the long hood and short trunk promised performance and power. The single headlights were mounted in square-shaped housings, and the grid-textured grille was simple and unfussy. The smooth-centered wheel trims were not popular with buyers and, in '71, prettier, chromed mock-wire wheels were offered. A year later, a mild face-lift saw a wider grille and vertical parking lights placed inboard of the headlights.

### REAR STABILITY

*Another option available, and fitted on this car, was rear antisway bars.*

### VINYL OPTION

*Black vinyl top was a $120 option. Buyers could also choose blue, dark gold, green, or white.*

### PILLAR

*Prodigious rear pillar made city parking literally hit-or-miss.*

### WHEELBASE

*The Monte Carlo was built to the smaller Chevelle's wheelbase, but was several inches longer.*

# 1970 PLYMOUTH
## *'Cuda*

THE 440-6 WAS A $250 'CUDA ENGINE OPTION

THE TOUGH-SOUNDING 1970s 'Cuda was one of the last flowerings of America's performance binge. Furiously fast, it was a totally new incarnation of the first '64 Barracuda and unashamedly aimed at psychopathic street-racers. Cynically, Plymouth even dubbed its belligerent model lineup "The Rapid Transit System."

The '70 Barracudas came in three styles – the 'Cuda was the performance model – and nine engine choices, topped by the outrageous 426cid Hemi. Chrysler's advertising men bellowed that the Hemi was "our angriest body wrapped around ol' King Kong hisself." But rising insurance rates and new emission standards meant that the muscle car was an endangered species. By 1973 Plymouth brochures showed a 'Cuda with a young married couple, complete with a baby in the smiling woman's arms. The party was well and truly over.

### INTERIOR
'Cuda interiors were flamboyant, with body-hugging bucket seats, Hurst pistol-grip shifter, and wood-grain steering wheel. This model has the Rallye instrument cluster, with tachometer, oil pressure gauge, and 150 mph (241 km/h) speedo.

### STYLING
*Plymouth stylists kept the shape uncluttered, with tapered-in bumpers, concealed wipers, flush door handles, smooth overhangs, and subtly flared wheel arches.*

### AIR CLEANER
*Unsilenced air cleaners such as this weren't allowed in California because of drive-by noise regulations.*

### SHAKER HOOD
*The distinctive shaker hood, allowing the air cleaner space to vibrate through the top of the hood, was a standard 'Cuda feature.*

### COLOR CHOICE
*'Cudas came in 18 strident colors, with funky names like "In Violet," "Lemon Twist," and "Vitamin C."*

### ENGINE
The 440cid "six-pack" Magnum motor cranked out 385 bhp and drank through three two-barrel Holley carbs, explaining the six-pack label. Base engine was a 383cid V8, which pushed out 335 horses.

## 1970 PLYMOUTH 'CUDA
The '70 'Cuda's crisp, taut styling is shared with the Dodge Challenger, and the classic long-hood/short-trunk design leaves you in no doubt that this is a pony car. Government legislation and hefty insurance rates ensured that this was the penultimate year of the big-engined Barracudas; after '71, the biggest block sold was a 340cid V8. By '74, total Barracudas sales for the year had slipped to just over 11,000, and it was axed before the '75 model year.

---

### SPECIFICATIONS

**MODEL** 1970 Plymouth 'Cuda
**PRODUCTION** 19,515
**BODY STYLE** Two-door, four-seater coupe and convertible.
**CONSTRUCTION** Steel unitary body.
**ENGINE** 383cid, 426cid, 440cid V8s.
**POWER OUTPUT** 335–425 bhp.
**TRANSMISSION** Three-speed manual, optional four-speed manual, and three-speed TorqueFlite automatic.
**SUSPENSION** *Front:* torsion bars; *Rear:* leaf springs with live axle.
**BRAKES** Front discs, rear drums.
**MAXIMUM SPEED** 137–150 mph (220–241 km/h)
**0–60 MPH** (0–96 KM/H) 5.9–6.9 sec
**A.F.C.** 12–17 mpg (4.2–6 km/l)

### PERFORMANCE PARTS
*Super Stock springs and a heavy-duty Dana 60 rear axle were standard on all 440 'Cudas.*

### STRIPING
*Optional inverted hockey stick graphics trumpeted engine size.*

# 1971 BUICK
## *Riviera*

THE '71 RIVIERA WAS A RADICAL MODEL
FOR TRADITIONALLY CONSERVATIVE BUICK

THE '63 RIVIERA HAD BEEN one of Buick's best sellers, but by the late Sixties it was lagging far behind Ford's now-luxurious Thunderbird. Even so, the Riviera easily outsold its stablemate, the radical front-wheel drive Toronado, but for '71 Buick upped the stakes by unveiling a new Riviera that was a little bit special.

Handsome and dramatic, the "boat-tail," as it was nicknamed, had its stylistic roots in the split rear-window Sting Ray of '63. It was as elegant as Jackie Onassis and as hard-hitting as Muhammad Ali. Its base price was $5,251, undercutting the arch-rival T-Bird by a wide margin. Designer Bill Mitchell nominated it as his favorite car of all time and, while sales of Rivieras hardly went crazy, at last Buick had a flagship coupe that was the envy of the industry.

### INTERIOR

Although the Seventies interior was plush and hedonistic, it was more than a little bit plasticky. After 1972, the rear seat could be split 60/40 – pretty neat for a coupe. The options list was infinite and you could swell the car's base

sticker price by a small fortune. Tilt steering wheel *(left)* was standard on the Riviera.

### ENGINE

The Riviera came with GM's biggest mill, the mighty 455. The even hotter Gran Sport option made the huge V8 even smoother and quieter, and offered big-buck buyers a whopping 330 bhp. One reviewer said of the GS-engined car, "there's nothing better made on these shores."

### PILLARLESS STYLE

With the side windows down, Buick's bruiser was pillarless, further gracing those swooping lines.

### SUPREME STOPPING POWER

The Riviera drew praise for its braking, helped by a Max Trac anti-skid option. The Riv could stop from 60 mph (96 km/h) in 135 ft (41 m), 40 ft (12 m) shorter than its rivals.

THIS IS THE
315 BHP ENGINE;
A 330 BHP UNIT WAS AVAILABLE AT EXTRA COST

SOFT-RAY
TINTED GLASS
HELPED KEEP
THINGS COOL

VENTS ARE PART OF THE AIR-CONDITIONING
SYSTEM AND UNIQUE TO '71 RIVIERAS

ELECTRIC TRUNK RELEASES ARE
NOT A MODERN PHENOMENON –
THEY WERE ON THE '71 RIVIERA'S
OPTIONS LIST

SEATING COULD BE
ALL-VINYL BENCH
SEATS WITH CUSTOM
TRIM OR FRONT BUCKETS

## OVERHEAD BEAUTY

The Riviera's styling may
have been excessive, but it
still made a capacious five-
seater, despite the fastback
roof line and massive
rear window. The 122 in
(3.1 m) wheelbase made
the '71 boat-tail longer
than previous Rivieras.

## CHUNKY REAR

The muscular rear flanks flow
into the boat-tail rear. Only a
Detroit stylist would graft a huge
chrome point to the back of a car.

WHEEL ARCHES WERE WIDE OPEN
AND WENT AGAINST THE TREND
FOR SKIRTED FENDERS

### SPECIFICATIONS

**MODEL** 1971 Buick Riviera
**PRODUCTION** 33,810
**BODY STYLE** Two-door coupe.
**CONSTRUCTION** Steel body and
box-section chassis.
**ENGINE** 455cid V8.
**POWER OUTPUT** 315–330 bhp.
**TRANSMISSION** Three-speed Turbo
Hydra-Matic automatic.
**SUSPENSION** *Front:* independent
coil springs;
*Rear:* self-leveling pneumatic
bellows over shocks.
**BRAKES** Front discs, rear drums.
**MAXIMUM SPEED** 125 mph
(201 km/h)
**0–60 MPH** (0–96 KM/H) 8.4 sec
**A.F.C.** 12–15 mpg
(4.2–5.3 km/l)

## EVOLUTION OF THE BUICK RIVIERA

THE RIVIERA TAG first appeared in 1949, when the Buick Roadmaster Riviera became the first pillarless hardtop convertible. During the Fifties, Buick spread the Riviera name all over the place, so, in 1955, for example, you could choose between a Buick Super Riviera, Roadmaster Riviera, Century Riviera, and Special Riviera. The name was so steadily misapplied that by 1971, the Riv had lost its special cachet and become just another land yacht.

### 1963

ONE OF THE ALL-TIME great automotive designs, in the same league as the '36–'37 Cord and the Continental Mark II, the Riviera was agile, sexy, and highly prized. The public loved it and it soon became the patriotic choice for Ivy League America. Even the Europeans raved. And with that 401cid V8 up front, it could even worry a Jag.

**KEY FEATURES**
- Standard 325 bhp 401cid V8 with optional 340 bhp 425cid V8
- Two-speed automatic transmission
- Open headlights
- Optional leather interior

### 1969

BY THE TIME THIS 1969 model hit the streets, the Riviera had gone through a number of rebirths. Headlights were hidden in '65, then exposed with a 1966 fastback redesign that lengthened the car, only to be hidden once more in '68. A GS (Gran Sport) option was introduced in 1965, and a larger power unit made available in 1967.

**KEY DEVELOPMENTS**
- Three-speed transmission from 1964
- 1966 redesign made car longer, heavier, and more curvaceous
- 1968 redesign of front view
- 360 bhp 430cid V8 unit available in 1967

### 1970

THE "NOW YOU SEE THEM, now you don't" headlights saga continued in this 1970 revamp; two years after they had been hidden away, out they came once more. Not that it did anything for the looks of the Riviera – the once "classic" styling had now been replaced by ugly retro design touches. A new power unit boosted output to 370 bhp.

**KEY DEVELOPMENTS**
- New 370 bhp 455cid V8 unit as standard
- Electronic skid-control braking system
- Now sitting on shortened Electra chassis
- All-new "E" body by Donald C. Laskey

## 1971 BUICK *Riviera*

VIEW FROM REARVIEW MIRROR WAS SLIGHTLY RESTRICTED

ONE-PIECE REAR WINDSHIELD CURVES DOWNWARD

DARING LINES SUCH AS THESE HAD NEVER BEFORE BEEN SEEN ON A PRODUCTION CAR

### CONTROVERSIAL STYLING

The rear of the car was a Bill Mitchell "classic" that had his trademark stamped all over it, the GM supremo having also designed the rear of the '63 Sting Ray coupe. This time, however, critics were not so universal in their praise, and even Mitchell found himself having to defend the design.

LAND OF ENCHANTMENT
AMY 589
72 NEW MEXICO USA

## 1977

AFTER THE "BOAT-TAIL" had been replaced by a more conventional design in 1974, there was little change until this downsizing in '77, which placed the Riviera on the same chassis as the new Electra. By this time, sales had fallen from nearly 43,000 in 1967 to 20,500, with the Riviera now regarded as just another standard luxury coupe.

### KEY DEVELOPMENTS
- 1971 redesign with radical "boat-tail" styling, blunted slightly in 1973
- 1974 redesign is far more conventional
- 1977 model downsized
- 455cid V8 has reduced output of 205 bhp
- "Mac-Trac" antiwheelspin system

## 1979

THE FIRST FRONT-WHEEL drive Buick Riviera entered the market in '79 on GM's newly downsized E-body platform. The body and mechanics were shared with the Cadillac Eldorado and Oldsmobile Toronado. Despite relatively minor styling changes from 1977, the public liked it and sales shot back up to nearly 53,000 units.

### KEY DEVELOPMENTS
- Front-wheel drive
- Sporty T-type with a turbo V6 available
- Disc brakes all around
- Lightest Riviera yet

## 1986

SALES OF THE RIVIERA rose in 1981, then dropped back in '82. The first convertible was introduced in 1983, but poor sales saw it withdrawn after 1985. The standard Riviera had a slight frontal design change in 1984, and this was the prelude to a complete downsizing again in 1986. Hardly a successful move as sales plummeted 70 percent.

### KEY DEVELOPMENTS
- Four-speed automatic gearbox introduced as standard in 1984
- Riviera convertible available 1983–85
- Downsized in 1986

## 1995

SALES HIT AN ALL-TIME LOW of just over 15,000 units in 1987, crashing to 8,625 a year later. Realizing that downsizing was probably not a good idea, Buick gave the 1989 Riviera an extra 11 in (28 cm) and a plusher ride; sales doubled. After falling sales in the early 1990s, this 1995 model harks back to the 1971–73 "boat-tail" era with its unusual yet stylish rear view.

### KEY DEVELOPMENTS
- Improved V6 in 1988
- 1989 redesign lengthened the car at back and added more comfort and chrome
- ABS as standard in 1991
- 1995 redesign with tapered tail and regular V6 (205 bhp) and supercharged V6 (225 bhp) engines

### CLASSY THROUGHOUT
The lines of the boat-tail were not only beautiful at the rear, but were carried right through to the thrusting, pointed grille.

### BUILT ON A REPUTATION
By 1971 the Riviera had become almost a caricature of itself, now bigger and brasher than it ever was before. It was the coupe in which to make a truly stunning entrance.

THE 455CID BLOCK COULD PUMP OUT 315 BHP AND REACH 60 (96 KM/H) IN 8.4 SECONDS

# 1971 CHEVROLET
## Nova SS

ONE OF CHEVROLET'S SALES TRIUMPHS

THE NOVA NAME FIRST appeared in 1962 as the top-line model of Chevrolet's new Falcon-buster compact, the Chevy II. Evolving into a range in its own right, by '71 the Nova's Super Sport (SS) package was one of the smallest muscle cars ever fielded by Detroit. In an era when performance was on the wane, the diminutive banshee found plenty of friends among the budget drag-racing set. That strong 350cid V8 just happened to be a small-block Chevy, perfect for all those tweaky manifolds, carbs, headers, and distributors courtesy of a massive hop-up industry. Some pundits even went so far as hailing the Nova SS as the Seventies equivalent of the '57 Chevy.

Frisky, tough, and impudent, Chevy's giant-killer could easily double the legal limit and, with wide-profile rubber, body stripes, Strato bucket seats, and custom interior, the SS was a Nova to die for. Quick and rare, only 7,016 '71 Novas sported the magic SS badge. Performance iron died a death in '72, making these last-of-the-line '71s perfect candidates for the "Chevy Muscle Hall of Fame."

**INTERIOR**
Nova features included front armrests, antitheft steering wheel-column lock, and ignition key alarm system. The $328 SS package bought a sports steering wheel and special gauges, but air-conditioning and a center console were extra-cost options.

**STYLING**
*The Nova's shell would last for 11 years and was shared with Buick, Oldsmobile, and Pontiac.*

**TIRES AND WHEELS**
*Wide-profile, bias-belted, white-lettered E70x14 tires were standard SS fare, but the handsome Sportmag five-spoke alloys were an $85 option.*

### PONY STYLING
*Playing on the "long-hood-short-deck" phrase used so much in Sixties auto-writing, Nova ads in the Seventies ran the copyline "Long Hood, Short Price."*

### LIGHTS
*Amber plastic lamp lenses were new for '71.*

## 1971 CHEVROLET NOVA SS

Handsome, neat, and chaste, the Nova was a new breed of passenger car for the Seventies. Advertised as the "Not Too Small Car," it looked a lot like a scaled-down version of the Chevelle and debuted in this form in 1968 to rave reviews. Safety legislation hit Detroit hard, and the Nova was forced to carry side marker-lights, shoulder harnesses, rear window defogger, dual-circuit brakes, and impact-absorbing steering column.

### BLOCK
*In '71, the option of a four-cylinder block was withdrawn on the Nova. Not surprising, considering that out of 315,000 Nova sales in 1970, only 2,247 buyers chose a four.*

### ENGINE
The two- or four-barrel 350cid V8 ran on regular fuel and pushed out 270 ponies. At one point, Chevrolet planned to squeeze the massive 454cid V8 from the Chevelle into the Nova SS, but regrettably dropped the idea.

# 1971 OLDSMOBILE
## 4-4-2

**INTERIOR**
Despite the cheap-looking wood-grain-vinyl dash, the 4-4-2's cabin had a real race-car feel. Bucket seats, custom steering wheel, and Hurst Competition gearshift came as standard, but the sports console at $77 and Rallye pack with clock and tacho at $84 were extras.

OLDS CHURNED OUT 558,889 CARS IN '71

1971 WAS THE LAST OF THE 4-4-2's glory years. A performance package *par excellence*, it was GM's longest-lived muscle car, tracing its roots all the way back to the heady days of '64, when a 4-4-2 combo was made available for the Oldsmobile Cutlass F-85. Possibly some of the most refined slingshots ever to come from any GM division, 4-4-2s had looks, charisma, and brawn to spare. The 4-4-2 nomenclature stood for a four-barrel carb, four-speed manual transmission, and two exhausts. Olds cleverly raided the storeroom, using hotshot parts previously available only to police departments. The deal was cheap and the noise on the street shattering. At $3,551, the super-swift Hardtop Coupe came with a 455cid V8, Rallye suspension, Strato bucket seats, and a top whack of 120 mph (193 km/h). The 4-4-2 package might have run and run had it not hit the '71 fuel crisis head on. Which proved a shame – because it was to be a long time before power like this would be seen again.

**ENGINE BLOCK**
*Oldsmobile never tired of proclaiming that its 455 cid mill was the largest V8 ever placed in a production car.*

**FRONT REDESIGN**
*1971 saw a new two-piece grille with twin headlights as separate units.*

**ENGINE**
"Factory blueprinted to save you money," screamed the ads. The monster 455cid V8 was stock for 4-4-2s in '71, but it was its swan-song year, and power output would soon dwindle.

**SIDE LIGHTS**
*Huge dinner-plate side lights almost looked like front-end exhausts.*

**442**

**REDUCED POWER**
Sales literature pronounced that "4-4-2 performance is strictly top drawer," but in reality, unleaded fuel meant a performance penalty.

### 1971 Oldsmobile 4-4-2

From 1964 to '67, the 4-4-2 was simply a performance option that could be fitted into the F-85 line, but its growing popularity meant that in 1968 Olds decided to create a separate series for it in hardtop and convertible guises. Advertising literature espoused the 4-4-2's torquey credentials: "A hot new number. Police needed it, Olds built it, pursuit proved it." But despite legislation that curbed the 4-4-2's power output and led to the series being deleted after '71, the 4-4-2 had made its mark and put Oldsmobile well up there on the muscle-car map.

**REAR DIFFERENTIAL**
*No less than eight rear-end ratios were offered, along with an optional antispin differential at $44.*

**COLOR CHOICES**
*In addition to this "Viking Blue," Oldsmobile added "Bittersweet," "Lime Green," and "Saturn Gold" to its 1971 color range.*

**EXHAUST**
*Apart from the label, the twin drain-pipe exhausts were the only clue that you were trailing a wild man.*

---

### SPECIFICATIONS

**MODEL** 1971 Oldsmobile 4-4-2
**PRODUCTION** 7,589
**BODY STYLE** Two-door coupe and convertible.
**CONSTRUCTION** Steel body and chassis.
**ENGINE** 455cid V8.
**POWER OUTPUT** 340–350 bhp.
**TRANSMISSION** Three-speed manual, optional four-speed manual, three-speed Turbo Hydra-Matic automatic.
**SUSPENSION** *Front:* coil springs; *Rear:* leaf springs.
**BRAKES** Front discs, rear drums.
**MAXIMUM SPEED** 125 mph (201 km/h)
**0–60 MPH** (0–96 km/h) 6.4 sec
**A.F.C.** 10–14 mpg (3.5–5 km/l)

# 1972 CHEVROLET
## *Camaro SS396*

AFTER A SUCCESSFUL DEBUT in '67, the Camaro hit the deck in '72. Sluggish sales and a 174-day strike at the Lordstown, Ohio, plant meant Camaros were in short supply, and only 68,656 were produced that year. Worse still, 1,100 half-finished cars sitting on the assembly lines couldn't meet the impending '73 bumper impact laws, so GM was forced to junk the lot. There were some dark mutterings in GM boardrooms. Should the Camaro be canned?

*6,562 CAMAROS HAD THE SS PACKAGE IN '72*

1972 also saw the Super Sport (SS) package bow out. *Road & Track* magazine mourned its passing, hailing the SS396 as "the best car built in America in 1971." But the early Seventies were a bad trip for the automobile, and the Camaro would rise again; five years later it was selling over a quarter of a million units. This is one American icon that refuses to die.

**CAMARO RACERS**
NASCAR racing has always been an important showcase for manufacturers of performance iron. Chevy spent big bucks to become a performance heavyweight, and the Camaro, along with the Chevelle, was a successful racing model in the early '70s.

**STYLING**
*The Camaro was designed using computer technology; the smooth horizontal surfaces blended together in an aerodynamically functional shape.*

**1972 CHEVROLET CAMARO SS396**
The Camaro design survived an incredible 11 years without any serious alteration. It lured eyes and dollars away from the traditional European performance machines and became one of the most recognized American GTs of the Seventies. In addition to the SS package, Camaros could also be specified in Rally Sport (RS) and Z-28 performance guise.

**WHEELS**
*Camaros came with five wheel-trim options.*

**REAR SPOILER**
*The SS and Z-28 packages got a rear-deck spoiler; the RS did not. The black rear panel is unique to the SS396.*

GNL 158
SOUTH CAROLINA

## ENGINE

Camaros came with engines to suit all pockets. The entry-level V8 was just $96 more than the plodding straight six. This is the lively 396cid V8, but the legendary 454cid V8, with a mind-blowing 425 bhp, was definitely not for the fainthearted.

## INTERIOR

Interior revisions for '72 were mostly confined to the door panels, which now included map bins and coin holders under the door handles. The high-back seats are a clue that this is a post-'70 model.

## GOOD PRICE

Individuality and power came cheap in '72 – the SS package cost just $306 – though extras were plentiful. Under 5,000 owners chose a six compared to nearly 64,000 who opted for one of the V8 options.

### COOL INTERIOR
*Air-conditioning for the Camaro cost an additional $397.*

### EXTRA GRIP
*Chevy dealers would even sell you spray-on liquid Tire Chain to improve traction on your Camaro, drag-race style.*

1776 Bicentennial 1976
GNL 158
SOUTH CAROLINA

## — SPECIFICATIONS —

**MODEL** 1972 Chevrolet Camaro SS396

**PRODUCTION** 6,562 (SS)

**BODY STYLE** Two-door coupe.

**CONSTRUCTION** Steel body and chassis.

**ENGINE** 350cid, 396cid, 402cid V8s (SS).

**POWER OUTPUT** 240–330 bhp.

**TRANSMISSION** Three-speed manual, optional four-speed manual, and automatic.

**SUSPENSION** *Front:* coil springs; *Rear:* leaf springs.

**BRAKES** Front power discs and rear drums.

**MAXIMUM SPEED** 125 mph (201 km/h)

**0–60 MPH** (0–96 KM/H) 7.5 sec

**A.F.C.** 15 mpg (5.3 km/l)

# 1972 LINCOLN
## *Continental Mark IV*

| Continental MARK IV | |
|---|---|
| ENGINE: 460 CU. IN. V-8 | OIL CAPACITY: 5 QTS. U.S. |
| CARBURETION: 4 VENTURI, 600 CFM | COOLING CAPACITY: 19.5 QTS U.S. |
| FUEL GRADE: 91 OCTANE (MINIMUM) | FUEL CAPACITY: 22.5 GAL. U.S |
| TRANS. RATIOS: 2.46/1, 1.46/1, 1:1 | ELECTRICAL SYSTEM: 12 VOLTS/85 AH |

THE MARK IV WAS LONGER AND WIDER THAN THE MARK IIi

IN 1972, $10,000 BOUGHT you TV detective Frank Cannon's corpulent Mark IV Continental, the luxury car fit to lock bumpers with Cadillac's finest. As big as they came and surprisingly fast, the all-new hunch-flanked body had a grille like the Rolls-Royce and distinctive, fake spare-wheel cover. Testers were unanimous in their praise for its power, luxury, and size, remarking that the Mark IV's hood "looks like an aircraft carrier landing-deck on final approach."

The list of luxury features was as long as a Manhattan phone directory – air-conditioning, six-by-six-way power seats, power windows, antenna, and door locks. And all standard. The air-con was about as complex and powerful as a Saturn rocket and, to please the legislators, under a hood the size of a baseball field nestled a forest of emission pipery. America may have wanted to kick the smog habit, but trim its waistline? Never.

### ENGINE
At 460cid, the Continental's V8 may have been Olympian, but it was still eclipsed by Cadillac's jumbo 500cid power plant that was around at the same time. The Mark IV block's power output for '72 was 224 bhp, a stark contrast to the 365 horses pushed out only a year before. Federal restrictions on power output had a lot to answer for.

### INTERIOR
Standard equipment included a Cartier electric clock, wood dash, and a six-way power Twin Comfort lounge seat. Even so, it all felt a bit tacky and didn't have the uptown cachet of European imports.

### SPACE AND COMFORT
A two-door in name, the Continental had room enough for five. The baroque interior is typical of the period, and the tiny "opera" window in the huge rear pillar became a Lincoln styling metaphor.

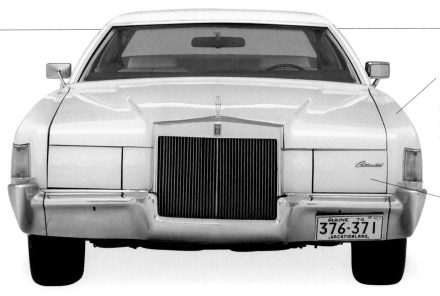

**COLOR CHOICE**
*The garish yellow is typical '70s, but all Mark IVs could be painted in a metallic hue for $127.*

**FRONT ASPECT**
*Shuttered headlights and heavyweight chrome bumper added to the car's presence.*

── SPECIFICATIONS ──

MODEL  1972 Lincoln Continental
Mark IV
PRODUCTION  48,591 (1972)
BODY STYLE  Two-door, five
seater hardtop.
CONSTRUCTION  Steel body
and chassis.
ENGINE  460cid V8.
POWER OUTPUT  224 bhp.
TRANSMISSION  Three-speed
Select-Shift automatic.
SUSPENSION  Helical coil front
and rear.
BRAKES  Front power discs,
rear drums.
MAXIMUM SPEED  122 mph
(196 km/h)
0–60 MPH (0–96 KM/H)  17.8 sec
A.F.C.  10 mpg (3.5 km/l)

## 1972 LINCOLN CONTINENTAL MARK IV

Rolls-Royce was mortally offended by the Continental's copy of their grille but didn't actually litigate. They wished they had because the grille went on to become a Lincoln trademark. The Mark IV offered more space for rear passengers and was the first Continental to incorporate an "opera" window into the rear pillar, albeit at a cost of $81.84.

**LEATHER TRIMMINGS**
*Leather lounge seats were an option at $179.*

**REAR EXTRAS**
*TractionLok differential and high-ratio rear axle were both on the options list.*

**ROOF**
*The vinyl, leather-look roof was standard on all Mark IVs.*

**CONTINENTAL COVER**
*This had been a Lincoln styling trait since the early Mark Is.*

**TIRES**
*Standard rubber was 225/15 radials.*

# 1973 PONTIAC
## *Trans Am*

WITH THE BRAWNY TRANS AM, PONTIAC KEPT THE BRUTE-FORCE PERFORMANCE FLAG FLYING

IN THE SEVENTIES, FOR THE FIRST time in American history, the Government stepped in between the motor industry and consumers. With the 1973 oil crisis, the Big Three were ordered to tighten their belts. Automotive design came to a screaming halt, and the big-block Trans Am became the last of the really fast cars.

The muscular Firebird had been around since 1969 and, with its rounded bulges, looked as if its skin had been forced out by the strength underneath. Gas shortage or not, the public liked the 1973 Trans Am, and sales quadrupled. The 455 Super Duty V8 had a socially unacceptable horsepower of 310 and, while Pontiac bravely tried to ignore the killjoy legislation, someone remarked that their High Output 455 was the largest engine ever offered in a pony car. The game was up, and within months modifications to comply with emission regulations had brought power down to 290 bhp.

The hell-raising 455 soldiered on until 1976, and that athletic fastback body until '82. But the frenetic muscle years of 1967–73 had irretrievably passed, and those wonderful big-block banshees would never be seen again.

### ELITE ENGINE
The big-block Trans Ams were Detroit's final salute to performance. The 455 Super Duty gave "the sort of acceleration that hasn't been seen in years." Reaching 60 mph (96 km/h) took under six seconds, and the engine could run all the way to 135 mph (217 km/h).

### ACTION-MAN MACHINE
The Trans Am was seriously macho. *Car & Driver* called it "a hard-muscled, lightning-reflexed commando of a car."

### SD ENGINE
The Super Duty V8 had cylinder heads that moved more air than Chrysler's famous Hemi. The 1973 455 SD could cover a quarter mile (0.4 km) in 13.8 seconds at 108 mph (174 km/h).

RACY FEATURES INCLUDED HOOD SCOOP AND FRONT AIR DAM, WHICH GAVE 50 LB (22.6 KG) OF DOWNFORCE AT HIGHWAY SPEEDS

### DASHBOARD
Second-edition Trans Ams had a standard engine-turned dash insert, Rally gauges, bucket seats, and a Formula steering wheel. The tach was calibrated to a very optimistic 8,000 rpm.

STANDARD EQUIPMENT INCLUDED POWER STEERING, FRONT DISCS, SAFE-T-TRACK DIFFERENTIAL, AND DUAL EXHAUSTS

THE TRANS AM'S SPEEDO WAS ONE OF DETROIT'S WILDEST, MAXING AT AN UNTRUTHFUL 160 MPH (257 KM/H)

### DECORATIVE DECAL
The "screaming chicken" graphics gracing the hood were new for 1973. Created by stylist John Schinella, they were a modern rendition of the American Indian phoenix symbol. Along with the rear-facing "shaker" hood scoop, the Trans Am now looked as distinctive as it drove.

### NAME IN DISPUTE
The Trans Am name was "borrowed" from the Sports Car Club of America, and the SCCA threatened to sue unless Pontiac paid a royalty of $5 per car.

ALTHOUGH BASED ON CHEVY'S F-BODY CAMARO, FIREBIRDS LOOKED AND HANDLED MUCH BETTER

### SPECIFICATIONS
**MODEL** 1973 *Pontiac Firebird Trans Am*

**PRODUCTION** 4,802

**BODY STYLE** Two-door, four-seater fastback.

**CONSTRUCTION** Steel unitary body.

**ENGINE** 455cid V8.

**POWER OUTPUT** 250–300 bhp.

**TRANSMISSION** Four-speed manual or three-speed Turbo Hydra-Matic automatic.

**SUSPENSION** *Front:* coil springs; *Rear:* leaf springs with live axle.

**BRAKES** Front discs, rear drums.

**MAXIMUM SPEED** 132 mph (212 km/h)

**0–60 MPH (0–96 KM/H)** 5.4 sec

**A.F.C.** 17 mpg (6 km/l)

HONEYCOMB WHEELS, COLORED SILVER, WERE A $36 OPTION

# EVOLUTION OF THE PONTIAC FIREBIRD TRANS AM

DETROIT'S OLDEST WARRIOR, the Firebird is the only muscle car that's been in the brochures for 30 years. Based on the Camaro's F-body, the Firebird debuted in 1967, but the wild Trans Am didn't appear until '69. Surprisingly, there was little fanfare until the hot 1970 restyle. Steep insurance rates and a national shift away from performance iron didn't help sales, but in 1973, the year of the "screaming chicken" hood decal and Super Duty V8, Trans Ams left showrooms like heat-seeking missiles. Nearly killed off by GM, the T/A soldiered on into the emasculated '80s and '90s – the only affordable brute-performance car to survive recession, legislative lunacy, and every gas crisis going.

A '77 TRANS AM SETS THE PACE IN THE MOODY 1978 THRILLER *THE DRIVER*

## 1968

THE FIREBIRD MAY HAVE shared the Camaro's sheet metal, but mechanically they were miles apart. With five different mills, from 230 to 400cid, the Firebird was a classic example of the pony car building-block philosophy: come up with a sexy-looking machine and then hand the customer a colossal option list.

### KEY FEATURES
- Introduced mid-1967
- Specially designed grille, taillights, and pleated seats
- Convertible available
- Firebird 400 has 325 bhp four-barrel powerhouse
- 82,560 sold in inaugural year

## 1971

THE SECOND-EDITION Trans Am had sexy curves oozing understated power. Quietly introduced in March 1969, the first Trans Am was sleek, sensual, and modern, and suited to only one body style – a quasi-fastback, which meant that the convertible was a thing of the past. The standard power unit was a potent 345 bhp Ram-Air III.

### KEY DEVELOPMENTS
- Body package has rear spoiler, front-fender air extractors, and rear-facing hood scoop
- New front bumper grille molded out of Endura rubber
- Softened spring rates
- Convertible deleted

# 1973 PONTIAC
## *Trans Am*

### REAR BUMPER
1973 was the "Year of the Bumper" because of Federal guidelines that rear bumpers should withstand low-speed impacts unscathed.

FLARED WHEEL ARCHES MADE THE TRANS AM LOOK EVEN TOUGHER

FOR 1973 THE FASTBACK BODYSHELL WAS GIVEN A FULL-WIDTH REAR-DECK SPOILER

### BODY BY FISHER
Pontiac wanted customers to believe that Trans Am bodies were hand-built by an old-time carriage-maker.

DUAL EXHAUSTS WITH CHROME EXTENSIONS WERE STANDARD

DLR **3055** D
MASSACHUSETTS

### 1992 DODGE VIPER R/T

*No other car packs the sheer wallop of the Viper. A 450 bhp V10, top speed of 180 mph (290 km/h), and jackhammer acceleration make this a four-wheeled riot. Coming showroom-fresh from a mass-production car maker, the Viper makes no sense at all. Which is why it's so mischievously marvelous.*

### 1993 FORD MUSTANG COBRA

*The late-model Mustang may not look like an emergent classic, but it has always offered a large helping of serious heave. Not for nothing did all those Highway Patrol guys choose the 5-liter as a high-speed pursuit machine. That high-output 302 V8 could crack the standing quarter in 14 seconds dead and hit 60 (96 km/h) in 6.5. That's quick.*

### 1995 BUICK RIVIERA COUPE

*GM stylist Bill Porter fielded his glam, all-new Riviera in 1994. A svelte two-door five-seater, the new Riv is more than worthy of the hallowed name that's always been reserved for a very special kind of Buick. The current model, with its sloping roof line and tapering flanks, proves that Detroit has always been able to sculpt in steel.*

### 1997 DODGE COPPERHEAD CONCEPT CAR

*A Viper of a different color, the Dodge Copperhead Concept Car is a '90s Austin-Healey. Eager to trade on their street-rod heritage, Chrysler has joined in the worldwide sports-car renaissance with a bang. With coil springs, a high-output 220 bhp aluminum V6, and five-speed manual, it's anything but just a pretty face. In an engagingly humorous touch, the tires have been given a snakeskin tread.*

### 1997 PLYMOUTH PROWLER

*Chrysler's wild child, the Prowler looks drop-dead gorgeous and makes a noise like God clearing his throat. And, believe it or not, this is a production car you can buy straight off the showroom floor. Beautifully detailed, gloriously impractical, it's a complete and utter wow, and proof that once again Chrysler is pushing auto styling over the edge and back again.*

# INDEX

1958 EDSEL CORSAIR CONVERTIBLE

1957 FORD FAIRLANE TOWN SEDAN

1959 FORD FAIRLANE 500
GALAXIE CLUB VICTORIA

1964 OLDSMOBILE
F-85 DELUXE